Second Edition, First Printing

Printed in the United States of America

ISBN #978-09826147-1-6 (hardbound)
ISBN #978-09826147-0-9 (paperback)
ISBN #978-09826147-2-3 (eBook)

Cover & Interior Artwork:
Pencilworx Design Group, LLC
www.pencilworx.com

Publisher:
RISING EAGLE PUBLISING, LLC
12138 Central Avenue, Suite 102
Bowie, Maryland 20721

www.jamesjosephwilliams.com
www.risingeaglepublishing.com
www.chasingtheeagle.com

CHASING
—THE—
EAGLE

JAMES J. WILLIAMS

From
Dreaming
to Achieving
Success & Freedom

FOREWORD BY:
GEORGE C. FRASER

TESTIMONIALS

"Chasing The Eagle: From Dreaming To Achieving Success & Freedom takes away all excuses from anyone who doesn't believe they can achieve both success and financial freedom. James Williams is a man who is not sharing ideas he has read about, but rather is sharing time tested strategies he has lived! I recommend you read this book and then re-read it. It will inspire you, empower you and impact you so that you will be able to live life at the next level! Read this book...you will be glad you did!"

WILLIE JOLLEY, best selling author of A Setback Is A Setup For A Comeback and An Attitude of Excellence!

"Chasing The Eagle: From Dreaming To Achieving Success & Freedom is a remarkable book, with practical wisdom for anyone seeking the fulfillment of a personal dream. An interesting read. James Williams has overcome incredible odds, putting considerable thought into this book. His experiences will inspire and motivate you to take action. Buckle your seatbelts. After reading this book, there are no excuses."

JOEL A. FREEMAN, Ph.D. author, CEO/President, The Freeman Institute®

"James Williams weaves an amazing story of struggle and triumph, dreams abandoned and fulfilled and the depth of character that evolves in the process. This is a must read for anyone who has ever reached, or wanted to reach beyond the present to the seemingly impossible."

LORETTA LOVE HUFF, creator of the RENEW My Life System™

"It is said that that which is most personal is most universal. James Williams captures and embodies the universal story of overcoming disadvantages, trials, and opposition to boldly realize your dreams. This book is a manual for achievers who want to convert their dreams into goals, and their goals into reality. The prerequisite to greatness is adversity, and Mr. Williams offers hope, encouragement, and humor to propel anyone toward a life of freedom and success."

LAVON LEWIS, CEO/President of Pencilworx Design Group

DEDICATIONS

This book is dedicated to the memory of my late father-in-law, Edward Bolden who made his transition with the Lord!

This book also is dedicated to you, the reader who dares to not only dream but achieve success and freedom on your terms. To you I would say that your success awaits. Now, go after it...I did!

Here's To Celebrating YOU!

From Dreaming To Achieving Success & Freedom

TABLE OF CONTENTS

Epigraph & Acknowledgements   *1*
Foreword   *3*
Introduction   *5*

SECTION 1: THE DREAM

Chapter 1: My Story   11
Chapter 2: Belief Through Quiet Confidence 17
Chapter 3: Taking Flight on Your Dreams   23
Chapter 4: Your Dream or Your Job?   27

SECTION 2: THE CHASE

Chapter 5: My Story   33
Chapter 6: The Pursuit of Excellence   37
Chapter 7: Failure & Disappointment   45
Chapter 8: The Importance of Not Giving Up 49

SECTION 3: THE ACHIEVEMENT

Chapter 9: My Story   55
Chapter 10: The Need for Achievement   61
Chapter 11: Managing Your Expectations   67
Chapter 12: Checking Your Vital Signs   71

SECTION 4: SUCCESS & FREEDOM

Chapter 13: My Story   77
Chapter 14: Success on Your Own Terms   81
Chapter 15: The Freedom of Giving Back   85
Chapter 16: Putting It All Together   89

ADDITIONAL RESOURCES   95
AUTHOR'S BIOGRAPHY   99

ACKNOWLEDGEMENTS

"Some people dream of worthy accomplishments, while others stay awake and do them."

- Anonymous

ACKNOWLEDGEMENTS

Thank you, Lord! You've equipped me to write this book.

To my amazing copy editor, Rhonda Larson. You are just awesome. Thank you!

To my parents who unselfishly brought me into this world against all odds. In particular, my mother who has always believed in my success & freedom, and made huge sacrifices to ensure I would get them both. Love you mom, this one's for you!

To my siblings, Dewayne, Gretta, and Rochelle. We grew up on the jagged edge of life and kept a sense of humor all the while. In the end, we did just fine. I wouldn't have had it any other way but with the four of us...love you guys!

To my late grandparents, Joe & Bertha Jackson who knew without a doubt that I would achieve success on my own terms. Grandma and grandpa, you were right!

To my military family of more than two decades. In particular, James E. Clemonts, Tyree E. Webster II, Kathleen J. Porter, Martin E. Pangelinan, John D. Croce and my fellow Army chief warrant officer (and friend) Virginia Oscovitch – I truly thank all of you. YOU ROCK!

To my career mentor, Jeremy J. Ross. Your insight greatly enhanced my professional career. Thank you, J!

To my closest friend of more than twenty-five years, Frank Malone. You and Lisa are the real deal. Thanks!

Last, but certainly not least, my rock, advisor and best friend—my wife, Greta, and our son, James II. You are the reason I continue *'chasing the eagle'*. Love you both!

WARNING—DISCLAIMER

This book is designed to provide information on dreaming and achieving success on your own terms. It is sold with the understanding that the publisher and author are not engaged in rendering legal, accounting or other professional services. If legal or other expert assistance is required, the services of a competent professional should be sought.

It is not the purpose of this book to reprint all the information that is otherwise available to authors and/or publishers, but instead to complement, amplify and supplement other texts. You are urged to read all the available material, learn as much as possible and tailor the information to your individual needs.

Every effort has been made to make this book as complete and as accurate as possible. However, there may be mistakes, both typographical and in content. Therefore, this text should be used only as a general guide and not as the ultimate source of information. Furthermore, this book contains information that is current only up to the printing date.

The purpose of this book is to educate and entertain. The author and publisher shall have neither liability nor responsibility to any person or entity with respect to any loss or damage caused, or alleged to have been caused, directly or indirectly, by the information contained in this book.

If you do not wish to be bound by the above, you may return this book to the publisher for a full refund.

FOREWORD

For more than 20 years, I've constantly preached the importance in performing with excellence. I want to point out that there is a distinction between "excellence" and *high personal achievement*. Our capacity for achievement varies according to how well we identify and expand upon our God-given gifts. It is human nature to concentrate on personal achievement as a building block of self-esteem.

Excellence, by my definition, is the reinvestment of one's unique gifts or personal achievements back into the community in order to improve the human condition within the community. It is my belief also that our generation must redefine excellence while maintaining high standards of personal achievement. This is our role and contribution. It is also the next step in our respective cultural development. For example: Magic Johnson winning the Most Valuable Player trophy is high personal achievement, and demonstrates success in his craft, but it is not excellence, not at least by my measure. The charitable work of the Magic Johnson Foundation, however is up to my standard of excellence in the African American community and also demonstrates the freedom of giving back to the community.

Whether you agree or disagree with the politics of the current administration, President Barack Obama ultimately defined "success" and "freedom" for not just African Americans, but "all" Americans. From a young man to well into adulthood, he was "chasing the eagle" in search of something much higher and powerful than himself. Ultimately, he was able to resuscitate the U.S. Constitution, particularly the passage "of the people" which has now been stamped to include "all of us".

In my opinion, there is no greatest success than living life on your own terms. Likewise, there is no greater freedom than the joy of giving back. The combination of success and freedom truly breeds a life of fulfillment.

Chasing The Eagle: From Dreaming to Achieving Success & Freedom is a must-read for anyone who has struggled to find a job, purchase a home, raise a child, launch a business, finish school, make a sale, get ahead, or do something extraordinary.

George C. Fraser
President/CEO Frasernet, Inc.
Author, Click: Ten Truths for Building Extraordinary Relationships

4

INTRODUCTION

First, let me begin by thanking you for the decision to travel this journey with me. My guess is that you too may have been at a crossroads in your life of defining success for yourself. Maybe you've had major success in your career yet felt a void in your life. Success without freedom, in my opinion is a life yet unfulfilled. Another way to put is:

SUCCESS + FREEDOM = FULFILLMENT

Over the past 10 years, I've had the pleasure of meeting very successful people. The names are far too many but there are a few that I've met that have had a huge impact on me. They are::

- George C. Fraser
- Dan Poynter
- Les Brown
- Fran Tarkington
- Harland Stonecipher
- Paul J. Meyer
- Dave Ramsey
- Willie Jolley
- Brian Tracy
- Jim Rohn
- Dr. Randal Pinkett
- President Bill Clinton
- The Whispers

Now I know the last set of names may have thrown you off, but those who know me personally are not surprised to know that I'm a HUGE fan of this musical singing group. Each time I've witnessed their live performances, I can only describe this dynamic group as magical! I once had the opportunity not only to meet them, but to have a group photo taken with them. I was so awestruck, that my wife served as my interpreter in asking for their autograph, as well as a group photo. She was able to translate my mute demeanor to them with ease: "My husband is a big fan of yours and has all of your CDs. He even sings some of your signature songs at local events". They were really cool with the whole encounter and obliged my wife's request. Today, I still have that photo with signatures from each corresponding artist. It was a great experience!

I mention the names above because the common denominator that they all share is that not only are they successful in their own right, but these individuals have a sense of freedom that is displayed in their particular craft.

Contrastly, I've met an equal number of successful people, including several millionaires. Their names will remain anonymous, but I can tell you that they did not seem to exude the same energy. I can only imagine that they had a mattress filled with checks not yet cashed. All the while, these individuals were totally unhappy and demonstrated what would appear to be a life of stress.

I once recall a mentor of mine articulating the correlation between success, philosophy and one's value system. He stated that having more money only magnifies who you are. The example he used was if a person possessed little money but had a drinking problem, having more money would ultimately send him to rehab. He would become more of what he already was.

The point I'd like to drive home is success is defined by who you are, but more importantly, who you wish to become. Would you rather be a millionaire or become a millionaire? I'd say the process of becoming a millionaire would be a character-building process vice just purchasing a winning lotto ticket.

After studying concepts of wealth and abundance over the last 10 years, I have come to realize how to create more wealth and abundance in my life, effortlessly.

I've read so many self-help books, attended conferences, completed exercises and have learned from some of the best "gurus" you may have heard about on *Oprah* or online. You may have purchased their books and followed their websites, but maybe you need more support to actually put their concepts into action. Now that they have become "celebrity gurus", the main challenge for most people is keeping up with the costs required to work with them. It can be worth the money you may spend. However, there are so many people who really want access to this knowledge who can't afford $1,200 – $5,000 to study with celebrity gurus. You don't have to. You already have the knowledge and I can help you to bring it out where it will be useful.

INTRODUCTION

I spent the last 10 years of my life testing the principles I will share with you. A budding author, entrepreneur, corporate professional, military officer, graduate student, husband and father, I have learned that anyone can have a life of success and freedom. I've conducted workshops, lead teams, and have carefully incorporated my successes and failures in this book. As for my failures, I don't wish for you to repeat them. This book also incorporates helpful tool kits, articles, and resources customized for the new business owner. I recently tested the tools and techniques that I created to confirm how quickly positive changes can occur. The results were a quality of life that I could not have imagined given my childhood experiences. I challenge you to put into action the tools you are ready to work with and see the results unfold in your life!

If after reading this book, you remain uncertain that you are ready to move forward, consider this: you have nothing to loose by choosing this path—you have much to gain. It depends on you!

This book is by no means a manual for becoming a millionaire for money spends very quickly. This book serves as a resource to provide you with the same tools that I was able to use to meet my goals and objectives. By the way, there were equally as many disappointments that I had to overcome to reach them. Likewise there were many victories on my way to reaching success and freedom.

Again, thank you for choosing this book to read. Enjoy!

SECTION 1

THE DREAM

Chapter 1

My Story

From Dreaming To Achieving Success & Freedom

The purpose of this book is to challenge anyone who has ever been lost in their path to their dreams. As a young man, I was taught in grade school that America was the land of the free and the home of the brave. I soon realized that our land is not free and that we are merely tenants. There is a cost that is not just monetary, but rather a cost of time and patience. Bravery as well as courage is what it truly takes to chase success and freedom. I believe that's the moment you've reached fulfillment.

The American eagle is our national bird that symbolizes freedom. That is something many of us pursue (freedom) in whatever way we deem that to represent for us. As a young boy, I was always fascinated by this particular bird, and had always aspired to soar with a wingspan that would stretch far and wide. As a kid, I would often try to chase the eagle only to realize that it was not how fast I could run, but how high I could soar. I apply this metaphor to rising above the adversity and hardships I've experienced. It is only when freedom runs through your veins that you know you've soared. That was music to my young ears. The chase was on!

This book is divided in four sections. Following each section, the chapter heading, *"My Story"* will follow (Chapters 1, 5, 9 and 13 respectively). My hope for you in reading this book is that you'll be able to use what I've learned over the past two decades to achieve your own goals. With that, let's begin!

To segue into the first chapter, the following passage introduces you to my journey to success:

The year was 1985, 25 years ago to be exact! It was August, the hottest month of summer in Cleveland, Ohio. I had just told my family that I had been accepted to Howard University and heading to the nation's capital. My only possessions were a few items of clothing, gas money for my then 1979 maroon Chevy Chevette, and a dream! As I pulled away from the driveway leaving the only environment I'd ever known, I witnessed my mother, grandmother, and my two sisters soaking the landscape with tears that could only come from fear of loss that this firstborn would leave the nest to *chase his eagle*. My one and only brother stood tall and said, "You'll do fine – stay strong." What brotherly love!

Fast forward twenty-five years, and I'm still chasing the eagle. As I write this book, it is summer of 2010. I sit humbly the on the island of Oahu in beautiful

MY STORY

Hawaii overlooking Pearl Harbor where I'm greeted by hibiscus succulents, pristine landscape and all the colors of men and women in uniform who are giving service to this great nation and living their dream! Success & freedom, there's just nothing like it!

Cleveland, Ohio...Where It All Began!

My ability to endure a volatile childhood, having less than most families, witness domestic violence in the household, and know that there were more possibilities outside my home environment ultimately shaped my dreams. In order to understand my ambition, you must understand my history and thus comes my story.

You see, I was initially conceived out of wedlock to teenage parents, Joyce Ann Jackson, and James Owens Williams, who were only 15 and 17 years of age at the time. The year was 1963, a time during the Civil Rights era where Emergence to Prosperity was on the rise—or so it seemed!

There are not enough pages to describe my mother, so there will just have to be a movie made about her life (Any takers?). She had a sanguine yet infectious personality that poured over into neighboring zipcodes. Born to Bertha Mae and Joe Jackson, my mother was the youngest of three children. Speaking of my grandparents, they are the two people who were most influential in shaping my world of dreams. They have greatly contributed to my accomplishments. They too were entrepreneurs in their own right.

My maternal grandmother was the financial wizard of the household, having managed a multitude of properties they both acquired over the years as part-time landlords. My grandmother had never been acquainted with an office job unless you account for her kitchen table where business was often conducted.

My maternal grandfather worked for a Cleveland lumber company for more than 30 years before a physical injury on the worksite would force him into early retirement. He was the epitome of genius—a true brain trust of his enterprise. Unless reading material was placed in front of him, one would never realize that he could neither read nor write. The running joke from my grandmother was that he only attended school three days of his life: 1) his first day of school, 2) to the principal's office for truancy, and 3) on his third visit, the schoolhouse was set ablaze. You could add that my grandmother inherited a comedic gene. All jokes aside, my grandfather had a temper that would make the devil himself flinch. He was notorious for scaring neighbors from the driveway of our home as they approached his property.

My mother had a fairly affluent childhood by most accounts. She certainly endured a great life in terms of food, shelter and was often the best dressed among her classmates. However with all those accoutrements, my mother always felt a void that was missing at home. Often when she felt discouraged, she would turn to her internal treasure chest. She was blessed with a special gift that would not be contained. That gift was her voice, and a songbird she was! She could carry any tune as if it were her personal handbag.

By age of 11, she recorded her first song on vinyl. That record which was yellow in color had remained in the family for many years. When we first heard her voice, we could not believe that was our mother singing. By age 12, my mother was approached by a local producer to attend a recording studio to further empower her gift. This would never happen for my grandmother wouldn't hear of her young child singing secular music.

And now to my father! My mother could only describe him as a vision of masculinity that even a blind woman would notice. She described him as a charming, street-wise young man who possessed an entrepreneurial wisdom far beyond his teenage years. He was truly my mother's first love. That love was confirmed when five months following conception, the three of us would levitate down the aisle at my grandmother's home. At age 17, my father hired a lawyer to legalize the marriage when neither of their parents would consent to it. Who would think to do that at age 17? On August 30, 1964, your author was born! By age 21, my mother would add my brother followed by two sisters to the eagle's nest. The Williams children wreaked havoc in that household you can be sure. One can only imagine the vices incurred for two young parents of four children. Lack of money, frustration, and even domestic violence would later earn the family of five the Lifetime Recipient Award presented by the Department of Health and Human Services.

I grew up on the east side of Cleveland, Ohio where conversations about wealth, college, and leaving the community just did not occur. Long before the city was deemed Lebron's town (Lebron James pro-basketball player), Cleveland was a blue collar town where the success of the steel mills, lumber and automotive industries would ensure a decent quality of life for the average family. My family would not be part of that statistic.

There was also the other side of life where your major employer was most notably, the Department of Health and Human Services. As long as you can show need, every six months you would be guaranteed your check each month along with food stamps, and health coverage. The Williams family would ultimately become lifetime members of this system.

I can remember my brother and me sitting on the lobby floor of the county welfare office. My mother awaited her name to be called. The humiliation for a 6-year-old to witness was criminal. The case manager, who I can only describe as a half paycheck away from being a public assistance recipient herself, would call my mother to her desk. Without losing concentration from the computer monitor, she would cock her M-16, load her magazine with rounds of questions, and fire away:

- Round 1 – "Ms Williams, why are you here?"
- Round 2 – "Why can't you find work?"
- Round 3 – "Have you been looking for a job?"

With one remaining round left in the chamber, she takes aim, and then pulls the $64,000 trigger question:

- **Final Round – "Did you graduate high school?"**

The tears from my mother's eyes began to soak the floor beneath her where my brother and I were playing. If having one child as a teenager could at least warrant the possibility of a GED, having four children would most certainly make this a pipe dream. My mother had a ninth grade education. The case manager made my mother feel less than human. Her insecurity grew as her self-esteem plummeted with each line of questioning. After about an hour of this interrogation, my mother was granted a $100 check and $50 in food stamps. So much for "chasing the eagle", for this brought on a whole new meaning. This way of life would continue until my youngest sibling reached her 18th birthday. Translation - our entire childhood!

My father had a need for achievement, and the societal pressure would prove too much for him to remain king of the castle. In his own way, he needed acceptance – self acceptance. This would require that he follow his dream to wherever life would take him. In this case, it was away from Cleveland, Ohio and away from his family. With that in mind, off he went! I personally thank him, because I'm a believer that absence can create as much of a positive outcome as it would a negative. His absence would allow God to come into our lives and shape us into His image. Today we are young men and women contributing to society in a meaningful way. We have all done well despite my father's departure, and we've forgiven him for it.

As a teaching moment, I want my readers to understand that while poverty is indeed a state of mind, it is not necessarily generational as most believe. In the case of our family, I could only describe it as, well—circumstantial! I'm sure it was never my mother's dream to live life as a career welfare recipient. To some degree, perhaps I've spent my entire life overcompensating for the dreams she never fulfilled. It's my way of saying, "I gotcha, Ma!" Actually, I stand corrected; she successfully raised four children through the trenches of almost every negative element imaginable. Perhaps if my grandparents had concurred with her pursuit of a singing career at such a young age, this book may not have been written.

Fast forward to age 10, I would often look out of my cracked window where my eyesight would take me to a place where negative elements included low income housing, and gang violence. A face like mine was considered criminal in certain parts of town. I was taught in grade school that America was the land of milk and honey. Well, in my neighborhood milk and honey were scarce. Wealth was based on "silk and money" from the neighborhood salesman. This was the guy who drove around the neighborhood often in a jet-black Cadillac and in the trunk of his car were silk ties, silk shirts, handkerchiefs and alike. His objective was to make money, of course. Thus silk and money!

I was incarcerated in an environment that was filled with narrow minds, and the thought of dreaming was considered strange. Escaping my circumstances was indeed a day-to-day fight. Dreams were the only luxury I could afford in my household for they had no monetary value but priceless all the same. However, looking through the window of my mind, my vision took me to places of humility where I could see myself as a success story going to places I could never dream of. I can tell you that I knew this day would come even at age 10, but it was up to me to give that dream a pulse.

Belief
Through Quiet
Confidence

I have to thank my wife for coining the term "quiet confidence" in our household. It is term she used often when describing my character traits and attributes. Quiet confidence is the ability to believe in what you're doing without ever displaying it outwardly – you just know it! More importantly, you're able to put your money where your mouth (or my case, mind) is. That has probably become my greatest attribute for most of the accomplishments I've made in my adult life. I believe in order to be a successful person, a display quiet confidence is sometimes necessary.

It is very important to turn within to see your vision. Oftentimes this may mean not sharing your beliefs with anyone to include your spouse. Now understand that this is a different concept than hiding a secret. This has more to do with limiting the distractions around you, even from those you love most. The outcome still becomes monumental, especially if those same people were supportive from conception to fruition of your dream.

I can remember receiving my acceptance letter to Howard University in June of 1985. At the time, I lived at home with my mother and siblings working full time for, now brace yourself...the American Automobile Association. Yep, AAA! I was that guy traveling across the country with AAA members anywhere from Bangor, Maine to Eugene, Oregon. How did I travel without petro or toll fees? With my bright orange highlighter and a map of the United States, of course! You might say that I was their tour guide on paper. Believe it or not, that summer job gave me an appreciation for geography that still exists present day.

I opened the letter and to my amazement, I was accepted to Howard University where I was to report to the university by mid- August. I purposely chose not to tell my family until the time was right.

This example may seem extreme, but I believe there are some of you reading this understand that sometimes the people you love can be your worst adversary without intending to be. As the oldest of four siblings, it was far time for me to spread my wings and journey to wherever life would take me next. I also knew that once I left the only place I've ever known, there would be no turning back. That really takes some time to ponder and I thought it was necessary to contain my excitement from the rest of the family.

BELIEF THROUGH QUIET CONFIDENCE

Overcoming obstacles with quiet confidence

Imagine working at your place of employment and your boss thinks he/ she knows absolutely everything. It's quite possible that they are very knowledgeable, having mostly what I commonly refer to as institutional knowledge. They make it a point to tell you in no uncertain terms that your career will go nowhere fast without their influence. Do you know people like that? Yeah, me too! I've worked in many organizations both in the private sector and especially my military career where this happens all the time. In the military community, in particular, it is your boss who has the greatest impact on your future success and career growth, right? Wrong! You are your career manager; however the people in the leadership chain of your organization may become the centers of influence. Your career may or may not prosper. This is where having a great attitude and quiet confidence comes in. So here are some action steps on how to exercise your "quiet confidence":

- Step 1: Do your research on your specific task at hand. Be very thorough in your research.
- Step 2: Know your task inside and out, but don't be boastful rather in a calm but confident manner and exercise humility where needed.
- Step 3: Ask the appropriate questions if you are uncertain, but only after you've exhausted all other options.
- Step 4: If at all possible, provide your final product before the deadline. My experience has been that under-promising and over-delivering seems to always please leadership!
- Step 5: Refrain from loosing your cool. Always maintain your professionalism even if you're not at fault. Having a negative attitude will only stagnate your development!

What did we just learn here? Through quiet confidence, you can achieve results in an effective and efficient manner without boasting, but more importantly, by having the right attitude (discussed later in this chapter).

Utilizing quiet confidence is not limited to your career goals, but in everyday use as well. For example, on average, I've achieved about a 93% success rate in rebutting denial letters from many vendors. This has been largely due to misrepresentation of my initial request or worse, misinformation all together. This still amazes my wife, so much so that I've often created response letters on her behalf. This can be a little complex because it requires that you keep excellent records from the start. This is another one of my greatest attributes. Ironically it is my wife who is the financial manager of our household, having been an accounting professional for more than twenty years. She's really thorough! She is very consistent with weekly reminders to me of "trash day". I always acknowledge her as the brain and I'm just the muscle in the house.

I once heard a mentor of mine state "If you stay ready, you never have to get ready!" Again, the key to quiet confidence is to know what you're talking about, and executing that knowledge when it's appropriate. The operative phrase is "when it's appropriate". There's no need to wear emotions on your sleeve just for attention or to demonstrate how smart you are. In the end, no one cares!

In recent years, the economy has taking its toll on just about everyone's confidence, regardless of status. However, there is an alternative. Do what you know well, or that comes easy to you. Initially, this may not necessarily mean you will enjoy it. However, during tough economic times, those inherent skills will keep food on the table for you and your family.

Before becoming a husband and father, one of my favorite past times was singing (I'm not sure where all this came from…any ideas?). In truth, I was an avid karaoke singer in my spare time. After more than five years of doing this, I decided to dabble into singing professionally. In this case, the opposite is true, I loved singing, but didn't consider myself a great singer. That is to say, I had no formal training, and I'd never joined a choir or a group at all.

I was your typical teenager who enjoyed athletics and had a thing for pursuing excellence. To be clear, I was a slightly above student. I'd say a solid B average (I was not a straight "A" student by any stretch). Now I qualify that by saying I was placed in the top half of my class and I excelled only when necessary. I've always believed in putting in the work to achieve the desired results. I knew this would please my mother for obvious reasons. As for my work ethic, I can only tip my hat to my grandfather who really instilled in my brother and me the importance of hard work. Today we are very productive citizens because of his teachings.

Singing, on the other hand, was a stress reliever and it gave me solace during those tough times particularly during my military service post 911. The interesting thing is that with each performance, my confidence shined

BELIEF THROUGH QUIET CONFIDENCE

and seemed to carry over quite well with the audience. Also, I was very intentional of the choice of song. Song choice matters because in my view, you're telling a story and in so doing, you're conveying a message though that song. This would be the only time this introvert would command attention from the audience because I had a story to tell. This had less to do with vocal talent and more to do with again, "quiet confidence".

Positive Mental Attitude

According to W. Clement Stone, author of *Believe and Achieve: W Clement Stone's 17 Principles of Success*, a positive mental attitude is "the right attitude in a given environment." It is composed of faith, optimism, hope, integrity, initiative, courage, generosity, tolerance, tact, kindness, and good sense. Positive Mental Attitude, or PMA, as it's commonly referred, allows you to achieve your goals, accumulate wealth, inspire others, and realize your dreams-however ambitious they may be – as long as you're willing to pay the price.

I believe this is what is keeping many people from reaching their dreams. For as long as I can remember, most of my successes have been solely based on my positive mental attitude.

Chapter 3

Taking Flight
on Your Dreams

From Dreaming To Achieving Success & Freedom

This is a challenge for most individuals. Many people take their dreams to their gravesite never to return (unless pursued by their offspring). I personally know many individuals who never pursued their true passion and would much rather take flight on their job than their dream (unless of course it's one and the same – a dream job). These are the same folks who complain about how unfair life is for them, and that the universe owes them something. If you know of someone who fits this description, do not shift your eyes left or right, please continue reading (unless of course, it's you).

In order to take flight on your dreams, you must first play the entire scenario in your mind. When I began to write this book, some 10 years ago, there were so many distractions just to get started. In the year 2000, I had already come up with the title *Chasing The Eagle*. It was more than a decade later before this book would eventually take flight. Why? There were chapters yet unknown, and therefore the book could not soar. I'm not suggesting that you wait 10 years to pursue your dream. The truth of the matter is during that time, I was dating my girlfriend (who later became my wife). We were both foot-loose and fancy-free having no children during that period of our lives. This allowed us to live life on our own terms. However once the marriage vows were locked in, it would be months later that we would become first-time parents at age 40. With that news, additional chapters of the book could now be written and the book took a life of its own.

There will be times where your dreams will lay dormant because of circumstances yet unknown, but as a man of faith, I know that everything happens in God's master plan.

Although your dreams may not take flight right away, they will happen if you stay focused. My dreams took flight the moment I pulled away from the driveway of my Ohio residence. There would be a thunderstorm of tears from my family once I broke the news that I would be relocating to the nation's capital. As previously mentioned, my only possessions were a 1979 Chevy Chevette, $100 for fuel costs, and a dream!

As I write this book, I still marvel on how it all came to be 25 years later. My childhood could never suggest that this would occur. In hindsight the only asset I could afford were my dreams. Food and other resources were scarce and family reunions were nonexistent for a single mother of 4 children. There were too many of us to feed! As the oldest, I knew that if dreams were to

TAKING FLIGHT ON YOUR DREAMS

happen, it was up to me to make them happen.

If the "why" to your dream is big enough, then the "how" will certainly take care of itself!

Prior to the publication of this book, I was invited to speak to a group of graduate students to share my story. I was speaking to a group of college students when one young woman told me that she had heard stories like mine so many times, and that she was an avid reader of books on fulfilling your dreams. Her question was, "What is so unique about your story…I've heard hundreds of stories like yours. What would make me pick up and read your book?" There was silence in the classroom, when suddenly the professor spoke up and said, "He overcame his circumstances and he's here to share his story with the class." The professor seemed annoyed by the student's question as if to say "How dare you question this young man who I personally asked to come here and addressed the class!" While I appreciate the interjection, I've come to realize that not everyone buys into this idea of dreaming of what you want and going after it.

The young lady didn't realize the answer lay beneath the question she had asked. My story is unique, all stories are unique. The difference is in the storytelling. I certainly captured the attention many of the students. Many of them asked me to return once this book was this published. In the end, the student was courageous for asking the question, and I acknowledged her question. I would say that it's how the story is told or in this case, written that makes the difference in how you're able to reach your audience. It's also ok that you won't reach everyone. I would encourage her to read this book before making an assessment.

Most individuals exist in today's society only to blame others for the circumstances that they put themselves in. They have not internally channeled what changes they would like to occur.

Unfortunately, I have found that many people have given up on their dreams, especially during these tough economic times; they don't even remember how to dream and therefore don't think they have a dream. However I have found that a dream mixed with confidence, determination, persistence, and massive belief will grow into a reality. The bigger the dream the bigger the rewards.

If You Can Dream It...

Mary McLeod Bethune had a dream. She wanted to start a college for black students who normally would not be able to attend college. She started the school in Daytona Beach, Florida, with six dollars to her name, but she was in possession of something more powerful: **A DREAM**. Today Bethune Cookman College is one of the great schools of higher education in this country. Moreover, Mary McLeod Bethune is remembered as one of America's greatest women because she believed in her dream and had confidence, determination, and persistence.

Dexter Yager, the former truck driver went on to build a multimillion-dollar business, and wrote, "If the Dream Is Big Enough, the Facts Don't Matter!"

Walt Disney said, "If you can dream it, you can do it." He didn't just say that to appease the masses. He said it because he knew from personal experience that it was true. Walt Disney started out as a simple cartoonist and went on to become one of the most successful entrepreneurs of all time.

James J. Williams made the decision leave his native Ohio to pursue his dream in 1985. Determined to chase his eagle, he set sights for the nation's capital. Twenty-five years later, he is not only the hero to his Ohio family, but is now a budding author, publisher, speaker and entrepreneur. However, James acknowledges his greatest accomplishment as his son, James II. He has now achieved success and freedom!

When will your dreams take flight?

Your Dream
or Your Job?

From Dreaming To Achieving Success & Freedom

This is a sticky topic that is often misunderstood, so I'll explain. I'm not at all suggesting that anyone reading this book should immediately quit their jobs in place of their passion. However, I've heard more than a dozen stories from colleagues who say that it was only after being fired from their job that their entrepreneurial flame ignited.

Sadly, we are programmed to believe that we can't have more. God forbid you already have a job and dream during these tough economic times. The stares from your neighbors, coworkers and even some family members may suggest that you're being boastful. If you exercise quiet confidence and not share these dreams with those same individuals, then the perception is that you're being secretive, right? So what do you do? First, don't allow yourself to be programmed! Your dreams are yours — to have and to hold, so own them!

Dual and Multiple Careers

If you're fortunate to have the "dream job", then maximize the opportunity that may someday you'll land on the entrepreneurial path to success! Dream jobs may not necessarily be cash cows, but if you love what you do then it's not really about the money, right?

For more than two decades, I've had the pleasure of having more than one career at the same time. Being both a career IT professional in the private sector and having a military career in the Army Reserves has been very gratifying. For the past decade, I've since added "entrepreneur" to that list. I don't' say this to impress you, rather to impress upon you that in certain instances you can have the "dream" and the "job" and still have other ventures—all going at the same time. No longer are options of having multiple income streams left only to athletes, entertainers, and people of wealth. This option has been available for centuries.

So that no one reading this book is left out - if you need to make a choice between a dream and a job, then be smart in your choice. You may have to work your dream part-time while maintaining a full-time job. There are only a very few instances where you work for the organization for 20-30 years and retire with a pension and gold watch.

YOUR DREAM OR YOUR JOB?

Your Job

It's important that you understand your value to yourself, not to your employer. Your employer will provide you value based on two things: 1) How well the company is doing financially, and, 2) The salary range for the position you are applying for or currently working in. It's that simple! I'm always amazed how many of my colleagues based their worth on what's on their current pay stub. You determine you're worth, no one else.

Having said that, there may be instances where a monetary promotion may not be the best career move for you. When being offered a position, you must consider all the factors. Remember salary is only a fraction of the compensation package. Let's just say you're a family of six. Would it benefit you to take less pay from an employer who offers an employer-paid health coverage, or would you rather take the increase in salary and pay a pricey monthly health premium? Did I fail to mention that the monthly premium may or may not include co-insurance payments for doctor's visits? It's important to weigh your options carefully.

This is where money management comes into play. If your expenses far exceed your salary, it really doesn't matter what your salary is. Living within or preferably below your means will insure a quality of life without financial stress. Again, don't make the mistake of allowing yourself to be seduced by a better job title or increased compensation. Likewise, be true to your worth as long as you can qualify it.

Your Dream

If you recall the example I used in the Introduction; money only magnifies who you already are. I don't mind telling you that I've been very fortunate in my career as far as compensation is concerned. But my humble beginnings kept me grounded and I've never fallen prey to the Hummer Effect (feeling invincible based on status while lacking decorum and rules of general conduct).

You also need to know which of your personality traits can help you in pursuing your dream. You may be an excellent craftsman, but if you cannot communicate effectively to a potential client or customer, you're dream could end up a nightmare. For example, I once worked with a colleague who was an independent contractor in the IT industry. He grew frustrated with his role as sole proprietor. After we talked about the source of his frustration, it became clear that he did not like working with people. He much prefers being a lone ranger and working behind the scenes. This attribute may not be a good fit for an entrepreneur of people.

In the end, will it come down to your *dream* or your *job*? In other words, do you choose to pursue your dream, or simply making money to survive? Both? That is the question only you can answer truthfully for yourself. For some, there may be more years behind you than ahead of you. **Choose wisely!**

SECTION 2

THE CHASE

Chapter 5

My Story

From Dreaming To Achieving Success & Freedom

In Pursuit of Value And Contribution

This section of the book is the core of how I came into my own. As mentioned in Chapter 3, at age 21, I left my native Ohio, and the chase was on. After the tearful goodbyes from the only place I've ever known, I would soon learn that this journey would be bumpy, with excessive potholes and several flat tires to include the spare. As it happened, I traveled down the Pennsylvania turnpike off to Washington, DC. Excited about attending an HBCU (Historically Black College/University), I was taken by the number of African Americans students from various backgrounds on a single campus setting. Having no family or mentors here in the nation's capital, my survival instincts had to kick in and fast. After all, the campus of Howard University was not located in some rural town, but in an urban environment. I declared that I would become a journalist.

I was a transfer student from Kent State University with a major in Business Administration (I was one of 10 finalists in my high school to receive scholarship funding). My initial school choice was Bowling Green University to which I received a four-year scholarship for Journalism. I chose Kent State because it was closer to home. After completing two years there, I eventually felt a disconnect from that university and moved back home for a year to decompress and ponder next action steps. It was during this time that I accepted the full-time position with AAA as previously mentioned in Chapter 1.

I was now a Howard University student declaring my major back to…you guessed it, Journalism. I was determined to become a news anchor, editor or publisher (or perhaps all 3). My experience at Howard instilled a competitive edge that I had not felt the need to have before. After all, I was public education product of John F. Kennedy High School in inner city Cleveland, Ohio. I felt I received a quality education. A once segregated school, JFK High became a culturally-sound school setting of students having coming led west-side and east-side students in the same building. I didn't feel necessarily the need to compete, right? Well, somehow I had this perception that many college students came from affluent, world-wide zip codes, while other students were continuing the legacy of their parents (for the most part this was true). More importantly, these students were VERY BRIGHT!

MY STORY

Prior to my acceptance to Howard University in 1985, just one year prior, I was accepted to Morehouse College in Atlanta, Georgia. For my readers who are not familiar with Morehouse College, it too is an HBCU, having graduated some of the brightest African American male minds today. Alumni like actor, Samuel L. Jackson, ministerial leader, Pastor Jamal Bryant, and the late Ennis Cosby who was the son of comedian Bill Cosby were among the alums. In 2006, Bill Cosby donated $3 million to the Morehouse School of Medicine — the largest individual endowment given to the school.

My enthusiasm was heightened after learning of my acceptance in 1984. It would later become deflated when my mother took ill and did not want me to leave Cleveland. You have to remember, I'm her firstborn child, and the expectation to manage the lives our my siblings was huge. She had grown attached. I suspect she could not endure another family member leaving the nest. The fear of loss kicked in for her, perhaps as a reminder of my father's abandonment many years earlier.

By now you've probably figured out why I kept close hold on the acceptance letter to Howard University the following year. I knew I had to leave. As far as I was concerned, there would be no further discussion.

Howard University was beautiful in every way. This environment restored my confidence to succeed, and by now, I had moved to what was probably the pivotal period of my life. I was in search of success and prosperity... or so it seemed. After two years of parties, campus activities, and countless absences, I found myself at a crossroads. I certainly discovered freedom, but had I achieved success? Not so much!

My housemates and I were to graduate as *The Class of 1989*. My excitement was certainly on board, but my grades were not good enough to get to my graduation goal. Could I have been overcompensating for being the man of the house since age 10? I knew that I could not get money from home to finish my degree, so what would I do now? My dreams of becoming a journalist were now becoming a distant memory.

Well, before I share with you the final outcome, I will say all seven of my housemates graduated on time and together in the same year, 1989. I was the only student whose dream would not be realized. If you can you imagine the failure and disappointment bestowed upon me, it was brutal. I could not share this with my family back home, not because they were paying the bill (remember, we had no money). They were betting on my success once I pulled away from that driveway. I certainly did not want to go back and work for AAA, although my performance was a guaranteed placement with the company. So I had to really dig deep and figure out where life would take me next.

The guilt and shame would force me to move out of the college environment. I was now a young adult man, living on my own in the nation's capital. I moved into my very first studio apartment. It would only be months later that I made a family discovery:

I was left to believe that I had no family there in the DC area, so I never gave it a second thought. Well, strangely enough I found my long lost uncle who I never met – until now. I would often see him looking at me from various billboards, but my tunnel vision didn't allow for distractions. One Saturday morning, we were finally introduced. And so the story goes I linked up and became yet another nephew of Uncle Sam and thus began my military career.

I walked into the recruiter's office because I knew of the GI Bill that assisted with tuition costs. My objective was to sign up for the Army reserves, fulfill my initial eight year contract while pursuing my Bachelor' Degree.

My only question to the recruiter was "Where do I sign?"

Chapter 6

The Pursuit of Excellence

From Dreaming To Achieving Success & Freedom

One of my mentors, George C. Fraser, author of *"Click: Ten Truths for Building Extraordinary Relationships"* always stressed the importance of conducting your business with excellence. He says that if you do a great job, you will compete amongst your peers when going to the next level, but if you perform with excellence, you'll have no competition. That statement has remained with me for over a decade.

There are some who view this type of pursuit as being an overachiever. Not you, of course! The idea of pursuing your goals and performing with excellence for some may be viewed as grandstanding. In the community where I grew up, this idea would be considered *selling out!* Each person on this planet is the CEO of themselves. Your character, thought process and your personal appearance are all attributes by which you are judged. Hiring managers also look for these qualities. Your positive mental attitude alone will get you much farther than your corporate blue suit.

Speaking of business apparel, here is some advice to my high school and college graduates, military retirees, or anyone in career transition to reinvent themselves. My advice: don't just wear the suit, be the suit! Be the confidence the suit represents. Demonstrate that through your assertiveness and confidence. I mentioned in a previous chapter that I like to sing. In order to reach my audience, I had to use my attributes not only to perform, but to win their confidence. Stage presence and song choice were perhaps my greatest attributes.

After realizing that I wasn't doing too badly at this singing thing, I decided to strive toward personal excellence and have fun with it at the same time. I would sign up for local talent shows; participate in vocal showcases where some of the best singers performed. An avid fan of *Showtime At The Apollo*, I would often say, "I'd like to do that!"

Strangely enough in the early 90s, a talent scout came to Howard University in search of 12 contestants to perform at the historic theater. My confidence was often challenged after seeing the talent from singers, dancers, comedians and stage actors. It was clear these folks were looking for a break and this was their way to get it. For me, it was an opportunity to strive for excellence in something I really enjoyed.

THE PURSUIT OF EXCELLENCE

Four hours had gone by and 11 names were called. I was just happy to have the confidence to challenge myself. I was grateful for any opportunity given. Well, "James Williams" was the twelfth and final name called. I couldn't believe that I was chosen over some truly great singers (By this time, I had taken a hiatus from pursuing my degree, and was merely striving for excellence in other god-given talents).

Weeks had gone by and I was off to New York for the very first time. There was a large white van for all the contestants. All 12 contestants and guests entered the van leaving the nation's capital eastbound to Harlem, New York. We got there, and to my surprise, the venue was much smaller than I had envisioned. Nonetheless, I was excited that I made the cut to perform. This was a 4 week journey in which the top three winners would return and perform until the grand finale. This finale would be called, Apollo Showcase of the Year.

We were advised that the song choice for each performance would continue each week up through the grand finale. In Chapter 2, we discussed song choice. I knew I had to "bring it" if I was going to make it to the final round. I also wanted to be original and not perform trendy songs just to appease this tough crowd.

My name was called to perform and I made sure that I was razor sharp head to toe. Thus, stage presence! The song choice was a song originally performed by the *Four Tops*, and later performed by Whitney Houston. You guessed it, *I Believe In You And Me*. Without question, my heart and soul went into this song. To my surprise, the crowd was receptive, and that performance would earn me third place, just enough to return for the next round. I would claim 3rd place for 3 consecutive weeks, which qualified me for the grand finale. I had time on my hands, since I was no longer a college student at Howard. Also during that time I had taken on a part time job, and I knew those earnings would not last long.

It would be on a weekday that I was to return to New York for the grand finale. That would not happen, and for a very good reason. During week three, I received a phone call to be interviewed for a position I responded to from a newspaper listing. This was a great opportunity to work for a major DC law firm. I would be responsible for billing and managing time and expenses for all partners, associates and interns. This position would allow me to use my analytical skills though I had no college degree at the time. After the interview, I was offered the job, and I accepted. I didn't return to Harlem for the grand finale. My move the nation's capital had little to do with talent showcases and more to do with academia and career advancement. It was fun while it lasted, but remaining on *Showtime At The Apollo* wasn't my ultimate goal.

As for the winner of the showcase, she was a young lady recently married and mother-to-be of her first child. She sang beautifully. This was indeed her dream. My dream was clear — my education. Remember my parents never returned to school after becoming teenage parents. As for the Apollo showcase, I was already a winner (three times in a row), and I was quite pleased with that. Time and place can many times set the stage for your life. I enjoyed my time, but my place was the law firm.

Why We Like to Be Busy

Have you ever noticed that most of us are constantly on a chase? We chase after many things, usually seeking the high that comes from a new object, a new feeling, a new emotion. If it's shiny and new, we want it whether it's a new gadget, a new buzz, a new love interest, or a new discovery. Ok, so what's wrong with seeking out new things? Isn't that fun? Shouldn't we be able to have a little fun? Yes, of course! The problem is when you seek out new things compulsively in ways that actually keep you from living the life you really want.

The Chase – Good and Bad

The *chase* can be a great thing that naturally drives us forward in life. It compels us towards our goals, meeting a spouse, having a family, starting a business, creating things, and more. It can also become detrimental when we don't apply forethought to our actions or pursue destructive ends. Examples may include overspending on things we don't need, getting involved in affairs, abusing drugs, and wasting time seeking out new and complex methods or tools when we already have ones that are simple and that work. On the last example, I think it is important to explore new ideas, but we must constantly check ourselves to keep this in balance. "Am I procrastinating, or am I truly in need of a new idea, method or tool?"

THE PURSUIT OF EXCELLENCE

How to Free Yourself from Compulsive Chasing and Live Your Dream Life

Compulsive chasing can often be a result of not knowing what to do next. Our goals are unclear, or unprioritized. Our life is full of physical and mental clutter so we try to escape this chaos through chasing the shiny and new. To stop this cycle I've put together a process to get you on track to clear out the clutter and obtain focus. To do this, I suggest taking one to two days off to organize your life. You may be thinking, "I can't do that!" Ah, but you can! Think back to times when you've been sick and couldn't perform home and work duties. The world goes on without us. So take some time for yourself now. You work hard and deserve to clear out mental and physical clutter so you can live the life of your dreams!

The "Organize Your Life" Process

The goal of this process is to declutter your world and mind, and then organize things, ideas, and goals so that you can live a purposeful life; one in which you are not just merely "busy" but engaged, excited, and living out your dreams. This process is meant to be modified by you so that it works best for you. These are just guidelines.

1. Prework: Read *Getting Things Done* by David Allen. I have a personal copy and it has greatly enhanced not only my organizational skills, but my productivity as well. Another great place to learn a similar approach is Zen To Done over at ZenHabits.net.

2. Tools you may need: In-basket, files, filing drawer or container, notebook, calendar, and just as important, a tickler or reminder file tool. You probably have most of these already. Please don't feel as though you need to get fancy. Simple is best when it comes to tools. These tools can be physical or electronic. Whatever system is easiest and most intuitive for you, use that.

3. First plan the big things you want to accomplish during your time. Examples might be:
- Clear out clutter in office (two hours)

From Dreaming To Achieving Success & Freedom

- Create places to put things to be donated, sold, or trashed (10 minutes)
- Organize papers, files, and reference items (two hours)
- Create plan to declutter whole house over next six weeks (15 minutes)
- Work on Goal Setting and Goal Implementation Planning and/or Goal Simplification (one to two hours)
- Take action on first steps of my top 1-3 goals (two hours)
- Plan my next steps -schedule it into calendar, tickler file or to-do reminder system (five minutes)
- Plan when I will do my weekly review (five minutes)

4. I suggest you "declutter" as a first physical action step. When in doubt, throw it out! However, don't get too carried away and throw out things that you really might need, especially if they are expensive. Simply find a "home" for those things. Don't aim for perfection, just aim for big progress. Don't let the little things bog you down. If you get stuck making a decision on an item, put it into your "review in six months pile" and move on to the next thing. Keep moving to make the most of your time.

5. Put stuff into piles:
- *Trash* (self-explanatory)
- *To be sold* (schedule in how/when you will sell this stuff so you ensure you'll do it. If you don't have a lot of time for this, either delegate that task to a local ebay seller or donate it)
- *To be donated* (load this stuff right into your car, or put near the front door if you're having it picked up)
- *To be reviewed in 6 months* (for things you can't decide on)

6. Organize your papers, files, books, things, and other reference materials. If items are associated with actions, write it down in your capture notebook and put the item in its place or trash if not needed. If items are reference, then file them or put them in their "home." If you need to be reminded of a reference item, put that on your capture list too and put the item away.

THE PURSUIT OF EXCELLENCE

7. Process your In-Box of papers and your Capture list. Assign tasks to projects, your next-action list (I still call it a To-Do List), and into reminder tools like calendar, reminder programs, or tickler files.

8. Goal Setting, Goal Planning, and Goal Simplifying. This will get you focused on how to live out your dream life. Check out these three guides for goal management. I suggest doing them in this order. If time is short, just do #2. (The guides are found on lifelearningtoday.com.)

1. Ultimate Goal Setting Guide + Free Download
2. Wrestling with Your Goals? (Goal Planning & Management)
3. Simplifying Your Goals

This exercise will take anywhere from 30 minutes to a couple hours depending on how detailed you want to get. It will give you direction and focus. You'll know what to do next. The clutter in your mind will be gone. You'll no longer be "busy" chasing new things for the sake of chasing, but rather you'll be journeying towards your dreams. This journey is the most useful way to channel the primal desire to chase. Eventually, I would suggest cultivating a shift in your perception from "chasing dreams" to "living my dreams."

9. Take action on at least one step you've identified in your goal planning to get the ball rolling. Plan the next few as well. This will make you feel great!

10. Commit to daily/weekly planning and periodic De-Cluttering.

• **Daily planning:** Plan your day realistically by assigning the amount of time it takes to complete a task. Then work your way down from hardest task to easiest!
• **Weekly Planning:** Capture ideas onto paper, Process In-Box, Review Goals, project lists, to-do lists, upcoming calendar, previous calendar week for missed items, and generally tidy up desk and other major areas.
• **Periodic De-Cluttering:** Choose a frequency that works for you and set reminders into your calendar. And then do it!

Chapter 7

Failure &
Disappointment

From Dreaming To Achieving Success & Freedom

This chapter is certainly one that I had to go long and deep with. Perhaps this chapter more than any other helped me redefine exactly what success and freedom was, but more importantly, what it was not.

Just weeks prior to completing my two-year military deployment, the woman whom I dated for more than seven years would say that word all men love to hear after finally having the nerves to pop the question - yes! There would not be an eighth year as far as I was concerned. Serving the military as a bachelor really placed perspective on the importance of personal relationships and family. My wife and I married on December 12, 2003.

This date became vitally important to us for two reasons: 1) the obvious annual celebration that typically occurs in traditional marriages, but more importantly, 2) it memorialized the mother-in-law I never had the pleasure of meeting. Her birthday was also on December 12th.

We were blessed to have been able to pay for the wedding outright without incurring additional debt. We had begun construction on our new home that we would move to in the coming months. Of most importance was that I was offered an IT Auditor position from my first employer following my two-year military deployment post 911. That was certainly icing on the cake.

Fast forward to the wedding/honeymoon; I had never set sail on a cruise prior to meeting my wife—it was a monumental experience. We set sail for seven days over the Christmas Holiday. Now I would become the *Warrant Officer and the Gentleman.* This was ultimate success and freedom.

In March of 2004, we decided to take a weekend getaway to New York to see the play *The Lion King.* This would be our second time seeing the play, having seen it a few years earlier in Toronto, Canada. We were excited to now see our first Broadway play together. Needless to say, the play exceeded our expectations. Once we returned to our hotel, I noticed my wife looked a bit under the weather – in a good way. An over-the-counter pregnancy test would confirm our suspicion; we would become first-time-parents at the ripe young age of 40! Upon our return, the test was reconfirmed by the physician.

As recent newlyweds, our excitement continued throughout the spring of 2004, as we periodically checked on our property lot. We were preparing for our new home and more importantly, our new arrival! As a married couple of

FAILURE & DISAPPOINTMENT

faith, we learned of an event in Atlanta, Georgia known as Mega-Fest hosted by Bishop TD Jakes, a world renowned preacher and spiritual leader. My wife and I were excited and set our sights for that event.

All was great at my place of employment and the staff was made aware of not only the good news of my wife and I as soon-to-be-first-time parents, but they gave me time off to attend the event. Life was really great for us, having just served my country, my wife, and now God along with tens of thousands of worship goers.

It's now the month of June and we're in Atlanta having the time of our lives, praising and worshiping together as a couple with child in the oven, as they say. We knew that our commitment to each other and to our Lord would be the driving force to a successful marriage and on the last day of the event, we reaffirmed that commitment to each other.

After a spirit-filled event, we returned home to our one-bedroom w/den apartment, climbing over boxes and eager to move into our new home. I returned to work with a smile ready to attack any obstacle that would come my way. Was I really ready?

Now comes the disappointment! I walked into the building and before I could hang up my jacket, I was asked to see the manager. Without going into details I was sabotaged by a technicality that I was unaware of. I was asked to turn in my badge and leave the building. The interesting thing was that I was calm and relaxed—at least at that moment. It was as if I were being fired by Donald Trump himself...

"Mr. Trump, thank you very much for the opportunity. It was indeed an honor."

My actual response...

"Guys, it really has been a pleasure, and I appreciate the opportunity."

Their faces were very telling to say the least, for I suspect they anticipated fireworks from me. As security was standing by the doorway, I shook the hands of both my immediate supervisor, and the Program Manager and gave a pleasant exchange to the guard as I made my exit. Fair to say, I left the building never to return.

Within each step toward my vehicle, the volume of my brain grew heavy – it was as if I opened the car door while literally standing on my head. By this time, it occurred to me what just happened. Now comes the painstaking decision of explaining this to my wife who is now standing by the door five months pregnant with our soon-to-be new child.

What must my father have felt to just walk away from a family of five at age 17? Now I am faced with a dilemma of informing my new bride, who was a career success in her own right, that her groom of six months is currently unemployed. With only months before construction would be completed on our new home, and more importantly months before our son would enter this world, this eagle chasing thing was starting to get eulogized and fast.

Chapter 8

The Importance of Not Giving Up

From Dreaming To Achieving Success & Freedom

I'm reminded of my grandfather who did not allow his inability to read or write keep him from achieving a great life for himself and my grandmother. My grandparents traveled every year without hesitation. I'm reminded of my hard work and late nights following a full-time job of writing papers to pursue the very best education I could have to prepare me.

There were times in pursuit of my dreams, where I had to ask myself, "What am I doing here?" I had been living in the nation's capital well over 10 years with no academic credentials to show for it. If I wanted a job, I would have been better off working for AAA with hopes of moving up to the Executive Level. That thought was quickly erased from my memory chip - that would not become my reality. So with that, I became a workhorse.

For many years, I had to adjust to the cost of living in the Washington, DC area. In my case, this required a few jobs at the same time. For three consecutive years, my schedule was weekdays 8 to 5, and weeknights 6pm to midnight Monday thru Friday. Let's not forget my military obligation involving one weekend per month. So once each month I would work 14 consecutive days and eves. Again, this went on for three years until the decision to complete my degree became clear. Fast forward to 2004, and now I'm a military veteran, newlywed, and father-to-be who is now unemployed.

I'm also reminded of a television commercial where the car salesman comes home from what would be his last day of a 9-to-5 job and says, "Honey I'm home...I ran out of gas...Lost my job... What's for dinner?" The joke was on me in this case, and so the story goes I entered our cluttered apartment, sat my wife down and began the discussion.

By this time, I became a bitter, angry, frustrated middle-aged man who felt betrayed by everything and everyone: my early childhood experiences, which made me feel inadequate that I could not compete in the workforce; my educational experiences which I spent more than a decade obtaining my bachelor's degree but yet did not prepare me to be as competitive as my Ivy League counterparts; and especially my employers, who I felt had conspired against me and were determined to deny my potential and limit my opportunity. Knowing I had just served a 24-month military assignment, recently married with firstborn child on the way would not sway my employer's decision to show me the door.

THE IMPORTANCE OF NOT GIVNG UP

Without procrastinating, I sat my wife down and shared with her what had occurred at the office. Her eyes truly said it all… "James, I believe in you, but I am a little scared" Ladies, if you're reading this book, then know that your belief in your mate is priceless! This is what I believe every man wants (and needs) to hear from you. That's certainly what I needed to hear from her. Billy D had it right, *"Success is nothing, without someone to share it with!"* (refers to the verbal line as portrayed by actor Billy D. Williams to Diana Ross in the 1975 film classic, *Mahogany*).

This obstacle would only strengthen my faith in God. Before her lips would part, I said, "Greta, we WILL pursue 'our' dream!" Success is what you will it to be, and I was going to make it happen. If reassurance was anything, then action would certainly be everything.

It was only a matter of weeks that I would not only exceed my own expectations, but the expectations of those who doubted my abilities in the first place. I was no longer that 10-year-old kid who had no control of his circumstances. I was now an assertive college graduate, husband and soon-to-be father, who had a dream to fulfill. I would not be deterred by one job loss here in the 21st Century.

To anyone who has struggled to find a job, purchase a home, raise a child, launch a business, finish school, or just get ahead in life, my advice is simple — **Never Give Up!**

Again, never give up! While it may seem simple, it's also easy to do—give up! I'm a believer in the human spirit and the ability of people to rise above their circumstances, their upbringing, and in my case, even their failures. It was Michael Jordan who said it best when he says he can accept failure, for everyone fails at something. However he cannot accept not trying.

SECTION 3

THE
ACHIEVEMENT

Chapter 9

My Story

From Dreaming To Achieving Success & Freedom

Achievement was something that had to happen for me. It was in my DNA. Some may view this as putting pressure on oneself, but for me, I simply enjoyed the challenge of doing the impossible.

When I finally became a college graduate, I also became a hero for my military comrades, as well as my family back in Ohio, of whom attended my commencement ceremony on June 24, 1996. After more than a decade since high school, how would I celebrate this personal accomplishment?

The summer of 1996 was also the year of the Olympics. This year was special—this would be the 100th Olympics hosted here in the United States. Namely, Atlanta, Georgia. Here was my chance to serve as a volunteer. With that, I applied to serve as an Olympic Volunteer for Centennial Olympic Games.

I had always been a track & field enthusiast having competed as a young teenager. In my neighborhood, I was known as one of fastest sprinters with flat feet. Although, I had a very fast take off, I would ultimately tap out after about 200 yards. During my military career, I would later learn that I had just as much endurance running long distances especially the Army 2-mile run. Likewise, I was an equally competitive swimmer. At the local YMCA, I was the guy to beat in the breaststroke, butterfly and freestyle. I could certainly hold my own. I suspect it was my quiet confidence!

Participating in the Centennial Olympic Games was a huge deal for me personally. Fair to say, I was all in. With literally millions (if not hundreds of millions) of online applications world-wide and just as many interviews, my application was accepted. Within a month of hanging up my college cap & gown, I had strapped on a new uniform as Olympic Volunteer. This opportunity was as much of a rush as qualifying in the starting block for the 100 meter dash. This was an unpaid assignment, but that was irrelevant to me. I was able to get permission from my boss to take leave for this opportunity and he obliged. With few exceptions, I've been very fortunate to be surrounded by great people.

I spent my entire summer in Atlanta. As volunteers, we were briefed, and presented with picture badges, and access to most of the events. Lunch was also provided for each volunteer. I served as part of the Technology team. As Data Manager, I was responsible for coordinating with a team of other volunteers, game officials, competition managers and the media. I had to ensure accurate scoring and placement of athlete data (in all 35 events) that would be downloaded, verified, and placed in the Worldwide Publication of the Centennial Olympic Games.

Following the commencement of the Games, all volunteers were given lapel pins and Letters of Appreciation for their service. This was most gratifying for me.

A Pay Raise from Uncle Sam

Almost ten years into my military career I was ready for upward mobility. By this time, I had achieved the rank of E-5, or sergeant which is the first rank of a non-commissioned officer (or NCO). My supervisor at the time was an E-7, or sergeant first class in the Army. This would be his last assignment before his retirement.

I was always ambitious about career objectives and always pursued excellence in anything I set out to achieve. Already a college graduate (thanks to the Montgomery GI bill), I decided to continue my second career in hopes of furthering my career. Becoming an officer was never something I considered. In part, I thought I had exceeded the age requirements at age 31. Also, I really enjoyed being an NCO, it seemed less political than being an officer. I simply wanted to graduate college, but I also wanted to give back (more on that in Ch 15).

I was always encouraged by many officer and enlisted personnel who praised my positive attitude and professionalism when in military uniform. One officer asked why I had not considered becoming a commissioned officer. After explaining to him my reasons, he suggested I put in an age waiver and apply.

Shortly thereafter, an opportunity for Officer Candidate School became available and I so I sought guidance on the process. As one who believes in using my chain-of-command, I approached my supervisor on the matter. My case was denied. I was told there would be no reason to apply because it wouldn't get approved. My supervisor possessed an ego the size of Peugeot Sound (and still growing). Always respectful, I acknowledged his answer, but I was also determined to explore other options for my career path.

From Dreaming To Achieving Success & Freedom

Fast-forward to 1998—I was still sergeant (since 1993) and going nowhere fast, I was approached by a fellow NCO who mentioned the Warrant Officer Corps. The requirement was an endorsement from the officer-in-charge and an application packet. I was unfamiliar with warrant officers, and there was no chance I would here it from my supervisor. I was also told it would be very competitive, and only a select few make the cut. That was music to my ears. Of course by now, you know I had to apply and make this happen.

In the months to follow, my application packet was complete with college transcripts, letters of endorsement, and minimum scores results from the Armed Services Vocational Aptitude Batter (ASVAB) Test. I packaged my application and sent it off to the Recruiter whom to this day— I've never met.

This was indeed an arduous task, especially when competing with other applicants who were as much as 3 grades higher in rank than me. In March 1998, I was accepted into Warrant Officer Candidate School. My supervisor was mailed a copy of the acceptance letter. Transitioning from enlisted member to become an Army officer was not uncommon, especially in a medical unit. Among my former enlisted personnel, there were mixed emotions for this was the first time in the unit's history that an enlisted soldier had gone on to become a warrant officer.

On August 7, 1998, following a four-week, mentally challenging, physically demanding and emotionally intensive course, I would achieve the rank W1. More importantly, I finally won the respect of my former supervisor who now had to respond to me as, "sir". Again, not having an ego, I thanked him for allowing me to serve under his leadership and it was off to my next reserve assignment.

On my last day, my entire unit, consisting of more than 800 officer and enlisted service members, honored me with a proper send off. The friendships developed and their belief in my potential success was very humbling. They expected great things from me in this new role, and I wasn't going to disappoint either of us.

By year 2000, my promotion from E5 to W2 was now realized. Uncle Sam rewarded me with yet another pay increase. To date this was the best decision I've made in my military career.

MY STORY

By now, you have probably figured out that humility coupled with quiet confidence reaps huge rewards. I readily admit that my humility which comes from my childhood experiences of having very little. I've always appreciated any opportunity I was afforded. That is an attribute I'm proud to say I took with me to the nation's capital. It has greatly impacted my success for the past 25 years.

My humility has often been mistaken as weakness, or soft if you grew up in my neighborhood. This is an official shout-out to my introverts out there – it's simply not true! In any case, that doesn't describe me in the least. I've always been a "go-getter", just ask my wife. When I first laid eyes on her more than ten years ago, my alter-ego said "Go, get her!" Today, we're a pair of happily married introverts with a young son who seems to have his own ambition.

While we're on the subject of ambition, I never understood this word "overachiever". What happened to life, liberty and the pursuit of excellence? In the game of life, it's competence that dictates your place on the planet. This has less to do with money and more to do with fulfillment. There are plenty of individuals making a difference without the title. However, if you're going to play in the game of success, you need to understand the rules.

My mother certainly wasn't viewed as an overachiever during her exchange with her case manager to become eligible for public assistance. I could just imagine the interview:

> **Case Manager:** "Ms. Williams, would you consider yourself an overachiever?"

> **Mom:** "Glad you asked. I was able to reach my goal of having 4 children by age 21, where most young girls are just completing a four-year degree by that age. As I see it, I exceeded my own expectations. What a great question!"

> **Case Manager:** "That's quite an achievement, you're just what we're looking for. My husband and I never had kids. Ms. Williams, would you like to have my job?"

Mom: "Thanks, but no thanks. I find the water much warmer on this side of life. Check please!"

Obviously, the imagined exchanged described above did not occur. This was a needs-based program for those applicants who fell into low income brackets. For us, there were no income brackets to trend or trace. Her need for public assistance was circumstantial. The question becomes, would relying on public assistance place a stigma on my mother as an "underachiever"? She could have easily put us up for adoption, or worse, chose not become a teenage mom at all through other means. Over the years, my mother has made a huge difference in the lives of her children, and all while having no major title other than Mom.

My Greatest Achievement

Of all the achievements and accomplishments made as discussed in previous chapters, my greatest achievement is being a father to my son. Even having earned my bachelors degree 14 years post-high school, and being honorably discharged after serving in two wars, they weren't the most important things after all. I had to one-up myself and marry my bride after a seven year courtship when many naysayers never thought we would. Those achievements I'm certainly proud of.

God and country are certainly high-ranking factors to me because I am a man of faith who loves his country. However, I believe that there is no greater achievement than family. If December 12, 2003 would be among my greatest achievements of marrying my bride, then that would only be followed by December 21, 2004, when just four days shy of Christmas we brought home our son, James. We were now both first-time parents at forty years old. Have I said that enough times? That is a book in and of itself.

Speaking of not giving up, the one and only dispute in which I was victorious over my wife was naming my son, James Joseph Williams II. For months, prior to his birth, my wife and I were tooth and nail over this subject. She felt the need for him to have his own identity. I indicated that by adding the Roman numeral II, he would. She agreed and the rest is history!

Chapter 10

The Need for Achievement

From Dreaming To Achieving Success & Freedom

Let's face it, we all look for recognition, if only for ourselves. It is what validates our worth and contribution to society. However, in order to feel that sense of achievement, we need to put some thought into how we can set and achieve our goals.

Goal Setting
There are five major factors that affect us:

1. **Environment**
   The people around us have a major affect on our daily lives. Our family, friends, and our workplace all have an affect on our daily decisions, emotions and perceptions. This is called, influence. We must all strive to create the most positive and uplifting environment around us as possible. This doesn't imply that our environment won't challenge us at times. But challenge can be good and often a necessary part of growth. Take care to surround yourself with the kind of people that will motivate, inspire and yes, even challenge you to move closer – not farther away – from your goals.

2. **Events**
   We are affected by events, some small, some large, some personal, some national, and some global.

3. **Knowledge**
   We are affected by knowledge, whatever we know, or don't know. Ignorance is not bliss. Ignorance is tragedy, devastation, and creates lack. Ignorance creates disease, and ignorance will empty your life. Ignorance is not bliss.

   Here's another good phrase to remember, "What you *don't* know *will* hurt you." What you don't know will tragically affect your life. What you don't know will leave your life empty. What you don't know will leave you without a relationship.

   We are all affected by knowledge, whether we know it or not. That is why it is imperative that you read books. Key phrase, "The book you don't read won't help."

THE NEED FOR ACHIEVEMENT

4. Results

We are affected by results. Whatever results you are currently getting are the harvest of your own decisions. Those are your current results. We are affected by those, whether it is financial results or personal results. Disciplines managed will render great results.

5. Dreams

Of the five factors, it is our dreams, our vision of the future, that are the most important.

Make sure that the greatest pull on your life is the pull of the future. Some live in the past, and let their lives be continually pulled and influenced by the past. And yes, we must remember the past, and review the past, and make it useful to us to invest in the future. But the key is to make sure that the greatest pull on your life is the pull of the future.

If you are slim on your dreams, if you are slim on your objectives and your purposes, if they aren't very well planned, then it doesn't pull very hard. Then you have more of a tendency to be pulled by the past, to be pulled apart by events or circumstances or to be pulled by distractions. In order to save yourself from being pulled apart by distractions or pulled back to the past, you must now start designing the future so that the greatest part of your attention and focus pulls you forward like a magnet into the future to accomplish your goals.

If you are weak in learning to set goals, or if you haven't really worked on setting goals, then it is a solution you need to consider.

Goals are like a magnet. They pull, and the stronger they are, the more purposeful they are, the bigger they are, the more unique they are. If you have excellent goals and high dreams, they will pull you through all kinds of down days and down seasons. They will pull you through a winter of discontent. They will pull you through distractions on every side that says, "Look here". Strong, powerful dreams, like a magnet, will pull you through those tough times. Strong dreams and goals pull you through a disaster.

Disaster swallows some people because they have nothing on the other side of the disaster to pull them through. A bad day can almost overwhelm you if

From Dreaming To Achieving Success & Freedom

you don't have something really purposeful to go for on the other side of that day—on the other side of the difficult time—on the other side of the down time. If you've got plenty out there to attract and pull, it will pull you through all these things. Learning to set goals is an incredible experience. Once I learned it, it transformed my life forever.

Four Stages of Consciousness

About 10 years ago, I became deeply acquainted with the 4 Stages of competence from a friend and business associate. This model has really helped me gauge and measure myself when learning new skills. According to this model, personal growth will basically allow your thinking to transform from unconscious incompetence to unconscious competence:

Stage 1. Unconscious Incompetence
> The individual neither understands nor knows how to do something, nor recognizes the deficit, nor has a desire to address it.

Stage 2. Conscious Incompetence
> Though the individual does not understand or know how to do something, he or she does recognize the deficit, without yet addressing it.

Stage 3. Conscious Competence
> The individual understands or knows how to do something. However, demonstrating the skill or knowledge requires a great deal of consciousness or concentration.

Stage 4. Unconscious Competence
> The individual has had so much practice with a skill that it becomes "second nature" and can be performed easily (often without concentrating too deeply). He or she may or may not be able to teach it to others, depending upon how and when it was learned

Native language is an example of unconscious competence. Not every native speaker who can understand and be understood in a language has the competence to teach it. Distinguishing between unconscious competence for performance-only versus unconscious competence with the ability to teach, the term "kinesthetic competence" is sometimes used for the ability to perform but not to teach, while "theoretic competence" refers to the ability

THE NEED FOR ACHIEVEMENT

to do both.

Certain brain personality types favor certain skills and each individual possesses different natural strengths and preferences. Therefore, advancing from, say, stage 3 to 4 in one skill might be easier for one person than for another. Certain individuals will even resist progression to stage 2, because they refuse to acknowledge or accept the relevance and benefit of a particular skill or ability. Individuals develop competence only after they recognize the relevance of their own incompetence in the skill concerned.

I found this information very valuable when applying this model. When I'm at a crossroads to something new that I've never taken on before, this is my preferred model. It is what often distinguishes those individuals who have a need to achieve.

Achievement is based on your ambition. Think of your achievement as a thermometer and your ambition as your thermostat. The degree temperature would serve as expectation management. We will discuss that in the next chapter. As you your ambition increases your achievements tends to follow as long as you manage your expectations. Unfortunately, I know several individuals who began their journey from hypothermia directly to cremation.

They are usually the type of individuals who need to be noticed, and will only go the extra mile only to demonstrate how smart they are. They neither regulate their temperature nor managed their expectation.

Find your need, focus on it, and you will achieve.

Chapter 11

Managing Your
Expectations

From Dreaming To Achieving Success & Freedom

The following article is sourced from Brazo Consulting and can be retrieved from:*http://consultingacademy.com/a08.shtm*

Remember when NBA superstar, Michael Jordan retired from professional basketball—again? That was a sad year for us NBA fans. Now, do you remember the excitement caused when he returned to basketball a couple of years following his retirement? There were quotes from every conceivable source, for months prior to the announcement: *"He's coming back." "No, he's not coming back."* Week after week, up to the day prior to the announcement. Imagine the pressures faced if you were Michael Jordan. Could you possibly say you were NOT coming back? You most likely could not. Michael's problem is an example of the law of expectations taken to an extreme (i.e. hype, the media equivalent of heightened expectations).

Welcome to the world of mind games: hype, spin, slant, innuendo, or whatever word you choose to use. When used ethically, this is also referred to as, "managing expectations."

I often ask participants at the beginning of our workshops what they'd like to learn. (This is my way of capturing their expectations.) "Managing expectations" invariably surfaces as the first or second concept. Why?

Expectation management techniques are very valuable in client service work. It's partly for our client's benefit - to keep their eyes on the ball, to work towards the same goals, etc. We also do it for our own benefit because our project targets are sometimes less precise than we wish they were. Our performance criteria are demanding and many activities, such as presentations or deliverables are frequent opportunities for clients to pass judgment on us.

Expectations cut two ways:

1. **They are a primary measure of your success.** In your client's mind, satisfaction is determined by how close you have come to their expectations, NOT how close you were to the wording of the contract or the scope of work or even the performance criteria.

2. **Expectations drive all of your clients' actions and decisions.** It's not their everyday duties or their "assigned role" or your very rational explanations that drive them, but their expectations.

MANAGING YOUR EXPECTATIONS

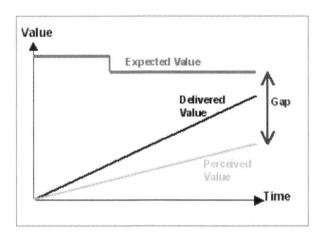

In the figure above, the red line represents your client's expectations, the black line a measure of the value you're providing and the green line your client's perception of that value. Notice the step down in the expectations line? That indicates expectations that have been successfully reduced. Perceived value is commonly below the actual delivered value, as the results are not always visible, not well explained or publicized. Your objective is to keep the gap between their expectation and the perceived value to a minimum.

My experience has shown that there are three components to managing expectations:

SMI: Set - Monitor - Influence
Any time I'm asked about an expectations problem, I respond with questions such as: "How was this expectation set?" "Who set it?" "When did you find out about it?" and, "What have you done about it?" The real answer is usually hidden in those questions.

1. Set Expectations
Expectations are set by all kinds of events. Whether it stems from something you said or did, or even the way you said it. It could also be something someone else said or did as well. It's important to know that expectations, rational or irrational, valid or invalid, are not developed in a vacuum.

From Dreaming To Achieving Success & Freedom

2. Capture/Monitor Expectations

It is not possible to know what the expectation setting is unless you actively search for it and continue monitoring it. You might even have to test it to see how it's set. Think of a power switch that doesn't have "on" and "off" labels. You don't know whether it's in the on or off position, unless you test it a couple of times. You can test expectations by dropping hints and clues of your next steps and watching how they react.

The old management adage says: "**You cannot manage what you don't measure.**" Common measurement tools are sales targets, league standings, satisfaction surveys, click-thru rates, and in project work, "percentage complete", and "estimate to completion".

The same adage can be re-stated for project work: "**You cannot manage expectations unless you monitor them.**" That requires listening to your clients and understanding them.

3. Influence Expectations

Once you have pinpointed the expectation and you know the source, it's time to work to influence your clients' expectations. This is what the experts usually mean when they say *manage the clients expectations*. Oftentimes they overlook the setting and monitoring components and expect you to talk your way out of anything. It's hard to talk your way out of anything unless you address the unmet expectations.

On the other hand, sometimes no influence is needed. Their expectations may be well founded, and we may be the one who need to change our approach and style.

Managed expectations will drive your success. Everything else is secondary. The SMI principles should give you enough to be prepared for your current client and future projects.

Chapter 12

Checking Your Vital Signs

Once you've made up your mind that you won't quit before reaching your goals, you will be driven toward the success you seek. However, you must develop some markers or milestones on your journey to let you know whether or not you're headed in the right direction. Doctors check your vital signs to determine the state of your health. You can even monitor a number of them yourself such as your heart rate, blood pressure, and weight to get an indication of whether your health is improving.

In business, companies use various measurements such as Return on Investment (ROI), Earnings per Share (EPS), and Return on Equity (ROE). These financial measurements become vital signs of their business. For the long-range goals you aspire to achieve, you need to establish some key measurements relevant to your goals. Monitoring these vital signs will help you make changes when necessary and keep you focused on the activities essential to your success.

Consistency

If you wanted, you could lose 20 pounds by a certain date, but the key to long term success is consistency. We can all change for a moment, but we must be consistent in our actions on a daily basis to produce any significant results on a consistent basis. Diets don't work because once people achieve their weight loss target, they go right back to the old habits that produced the weight gain in the first place. The only way to permanently stay fit is to develop healthy lifestyle habits and practice them for a lifetime. Being consistent in your actions will allow you to continually perform at a high level.

It's been said that "the race won is not to the swift, nor the strong, but to those who endure." Develop the mindset that looks at the success as a long-term proposition. Commit yourself to sustaining your performance as long as it takes to win. Even after reaching your objective, you'll set a higher goal because you've developed the habit of winning. Mastering the art of consistency will set you apart from those who work when they feel like it.

A few years ago I went to the dentist office for a routine teeth cleaning. I was greeted by the dental hygienist and I was her first appointment. As I sat in the chair, and after about ten minutes she began complaining about being there. It was only half past 8am, and already she had indicated that this was a bad day for her to come to work. I was concerned that my teeth would become

CHECKING YOUR VITAL SIGNS

the object of her frustration. Would I leave the office wearing a smile or veneers? Months later I returned for another cleaning and to my surprise she was no longer there (I say this sarcastically, of course). Her only consistency was that she stayed away from the office.

I once heard of a story of a spectator who attended a concert. After a riveting concert performance, an admiring fan said to the master violinist, "I would give my life to play like you." After a moment of reflection, the violinist quietly said, "Sir, that is what it would take. I have given my life to play like me." Goals are simple vehicles that allow you to express more of who you are. Consistency in the pursuit of those goals help you to realize more of your potential.

Life Vital Signs

The most obvious benefit to actively nurturing your own health and physical wellness is of course a significant increase in the likelihood of remaining healthy, catching and treating evolving health issues or problems early. Thus reducing the chances of serious problems developing or becoming worse and increasing the chances of a longer life of optimum health.

Let's take this wellness concept a step further and apply the concept of a check-up to how you are living your life in a more universal sense. Here are some questions you should ponder:

- Are you living a balanced life of intention and purpose?

- Do you have a clear set of goals written down (which you can articulate, if asked) to support incremental progress and achievement of the priorities and dreams you've defined for your life?

- Do you have a clear sense of direction and meaning to the manner in which you are living and how you are allocating your time, energy and God-given talents in key areas of life? (Faith, career, family, social relationships, community involvement, etc)

If you don't have the peace that comes from a clear sense of purpose and balance in your life, let me share some great news: you have the power to take action and become fully engaged in your own life, which is likely to

From Dreaming To Achieving Success & Freedom

give you a strange, yet wonderful combination of zestful energy to fuel the achievement of your goals and dreams, while also creating a sense of peace that only comes from a life of purposeful intention. The wheel below depicts categories in life that should be purposed and balanced to achieve your own ideal steady state:

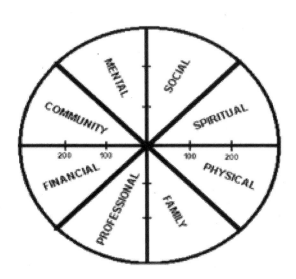

What are your thoughts as you reflect on the vital signs of your life right now based on the quick inventory above? Do you feel your life is in balance overall across key components of your life?

If you are tracking in synchronization with your dreams and following your calling, with a strong sense of clarity, purpose and joy in key areas of your life, then let me congratulate you!

SECTION 4

SUCCESS
& FREEDOM

Chapter 13

My Story

"Money won't create success, the freedom to make it will."
- Nelson Mandela

I could not think of a better way to define success and freedom in one sentence without mentioning the man who pioneered both, Nelson Mandela. He is by far one of the most admired and revered political leaders in the world.

Nelson Mandela was the first person in his family to receive a formal education. As a young lawyer in Johannesburg, South Africa, Mandela became increasingly involved in the African National Congress, which sought to unite all Africans and restore their rights. He was heavily involved in boycotts and mobilizing citizens, eventually being accused of treason and sentenced to life in prison. After nearly 30 years behind bars, Mandela was released and elected as the first black president of South Africa, in 1994. He continues to be a force on numerous issues, including AIDs, poverty and human rights. For his work, Mandela received the prestigious Nobel Peace Prize, among many other awards. In my view this truly defines success and freedom.

Hawaiian Summer of 2010

Two thousand and ten has proven to be a remarkable year for me and my family. That summer, we had the ultimate summer experience. I was given the good fortune to take a military assignment while spending the entire summer with my family. For more than 90 days, I would be awakened by a strong presence of Diamond Head (located in the heart of Waikiki on the island of Oahu in Hawaii). Each duty day, I would leave my quarters where my wife and son would remain asleep. Each morning, they, too, would be awakened by the same physical structure which was visible from the lanai.

There's something to be said about success and freedom. I enjoy my military time so much that I never once considered it to be work at all. Very often I would work as early as 6 am and as late as 8 pm. Since there was only one vehicle, I would drive into my location. Waikiki would be considered home for the summer. My son made sandcastles, and my wife made reservations. My son would go to places like the petting zoo, aquarium, the Children's museum and Sea Life Park. As for wife, shopping of course! My son picked seashells, and starfish and my wife picked shoes, jewelry, and lots of sundresses.

MY STORY

The freedom of knowing that they could pick a tourist attraction of their choosing was added peace of mind. Before returning to the mainland, we had the opportunity to go to the island of Maui. This four day weekend would be my only time of relaxation during the 3-month tour of duty. It was well worth it. We occupied a resort in Kihei, a town on the south side of the island. Of course, we weren't limited to that location. Our four day weekend excursion included beach walks, good food, and for my wife, you guessed it – shopping! However the best was yet to come.

I explored my adventurous side by ziplining at world famous Piiholo Ranch. This was a solo trip. My son was far too young and my wife is not huge fan of high places. It was a breathtaking experience being suspending in midair, while cruising as far 2800 feet across the valley. For about 90 seconds, I zipped past fruit and nut trees that were nestled in between the very green rainforest. This experience would only be followed by the big finale.

On our last day in Maui, the three of us took a helicopter to West Maui and Molokai. With my son in the front seat and my wife taken by the green colors from the side window view, we witnessed deep, meandering valleys set in the rainforest of the ancient West Maui Mountains along with knife-edged ridges with mist-shrouded peaks that separate the spectacular valleys. Imagine the Waterfalls cascading down from towering cliffs into the streams that ran along the rainforest floor. We saw the famous Iao valley and learned about the history of the sights from the pilot, who is also a certified tour guide. The tour was near completion as we crossed the Pailolo Channel to the "Friendly Isle." Molokai has the world's highest, most spectacular sea cliffs. That coupled with the island's tallest waterfall, remote valleys and the famous Kalaupapa peninsula was panoramic. The end! Can you imagine this? It's an experience we'll never forget.

By late August, my family returned to the mainland. My son was preparing for Kindergarten. I remained on the island until late September. I was not able to physically see my son off on his first day of school. Electronically, I was merely keystrokes away.

The six hour time difference did not deter my commitment to see my son off to his first day of Kindergarten. I had awakened at 1 am, Hawaii Time. James rose for school at the same time of 7 am EST. Through my computer screen, I could see him sitting on the table eating breakfast. Unaware what would happen next, his mother motioned him to look on the laptop screen. The look in his eyes once he saw his old man's face on the screen was priceless! Thanks to Skype, I was able to see him off to school. I believe his fondest memories of creative time spent with me will far outlast his Star Wars gadgets. It is my belief that the greatest gift to a child is the gift of great memories.

How am I able to live life in abundance with my family? It comes from a decision I made to no longer live by someone else's rules or timetable. I still maintain my primary career as well as my second career with the military all while pursuing doctoral studies. Balancing family, career, and graduate school is no easy task, but it has proven to be the key to my success in having a great life. That is far more valuable to than chasing a salary. I'm not driven by money itself, but the quality of life enhancement it offers.

The great thing about being an entrepreneur is that you are NOT ALONE. When you take responsibility for your life, you tend to link-up with other like-minded people who are more than willing to assist. Success breeds success, and successful people were once in the same place you are. They know what it took to make a change and how scary that was. They also know how to help you – so ask for help! Thankfully I'm in a business that has also attracted very successful people who I am continuing to learn from. There's nothing wrong with asking for help, as long as you're learning how to do it, not expecting someone else to do the work for you.

Change, freedom and self-reliance is available to absolutely anyone but you've got to want it badly enough or the first hurdle you face will be enough to break your resolve and send you back to your comfort zone.

Chapter 14

Success on Your Own Terms

I've studied success principles for more than a decade. Now I'm a budding author and publisher and I enjoy what I do. What's more; I love the fact that I can offer others the chance to live like my family and I live. Now, everyone loves the idea of having more money, more freedom and more success, but not everyone is willing to put in the work to achieve it. That's why more than 90% of the population 'just get by'. I found the solution to my family's needs that also helps others in the process. That's pretty powerful.

Defining Success for Yourself

I want to be clear that defining success for yourself doesn't not mean becoming arrogant against the establishment who may have set you on the path to that definition. By the same token, it is important that you define your strengths and weaknesses. If someone else discovers them first, that only leaves room for you to become bait for the organization.

This is the organization that will dictate your time, value and worth. While I enjoy serving in uniform, I never particularly cared for the politics involve (though I acknowledge it). The occurrence I mentioned in a previous chapter on my supervisor's unwillingness to enhance my military career is just one example of this. In the military community, your skin will be tested for toughness. So again, know yourself, first.

Financial Success

Most people would agree that they crave one or more of these three things at any one time: Money, freedom and success. The first two go hand in hand. When you have money, you have freedom. I don't believe you can have freedom without money because we live in an "exchange society". To get the things you need to live you either have to give your time or your money – that's not freedom. Having money frees up your time and allows you to do the things you want at any time – that's freedom. Everyone would like more freedom to do what brings them joy. Success is a different matter altogether in part because it means vastly different things to each individual. Whatever success means to you, I bet you'd like more of that too.

There's nothing wrong with wanting more. Unfortunately, wanting more money is often frowned upon because it is somehow viewed as being

SUCCESS ON YOUR OWN TERMS

"greedy". I respectfully disagree. If you really want to help others, it'll help if you have the freedom to do so. Taking care of the financial piece will enable you to help others more, right? Well, what if I told you that I've found a way of doing that? In fact it takes care of all three of the basic human desires I've written about here--more money, more time and more freedom.

Freedom is a cool thing: it allows me to spend more time on being a dad, and investing in my relationship with my son. It enables me to decide for myself what I do with my day, everyday. I wouldn't have any of that if I didn't make the choice to be a business owner. I know I'm in the right business because I'm helping others who need help AND I'm helping others start their own business here so they can be a solution for themselves and others too.

If you'd like to be a solution – then congratulations you are on the path to success & freedom!

Successful Relationships

As George C. Fraser points out in his book *Click: Ten Truths for Building Extraordinary Relationships*, the important relationships in your life are generally with a spouse, business partner or friend requires commitment. I agree with him, and I take every opportunity to cultivate happiness and trust in these relationships.

I cannot tell you how many times I've handed out business cards to individuals, literally hundred and never hear from them again. Once upon a time, I was the lone ranger myself, so I understand that building relationships takes time. For most men, this is easy to do only where sports, politics and the military are concerned. Beyond that, it's virtually no dice!

For many women on the other hand, they can practically start a conversation on Skype for the first time, and instantly connect for Happy Hour using social media within the hour. I believe both gender and personality play an important part in this. If you're a Type A personality, you can serve as your own free agent and would do well in succeeding on your terms, because you may have already mapped out a blueprint.

However we mustn't rule out the introverts. A self-proclaimed introvert myself, I always knew exactly what I wanted and aligned my thoughts and actions with that decision. It would be a mistake to believe that the soft-spoken cannot chart their course in life. I've met many introverted men and women who away from the office are making great strides in their communities and are well respected among their peers.

In the end, a happy relationship results in a happy life!

Chapter 15

The Freedom
of Giving Back

From Dreaming To Achieving Success & Freedom

One of the great things about achieving success is that you get the chance to give back to help others who may not be so fortunate. I once read an article about Richard Branson, a man whose entrepreneurial spirit knows no boundaries. He's the guy who coined the phrase "screw it – let's do it" which really epitomizes the thought that risks must be taken in order for progress to happen.

A few years ago, the teenager and later mother if 4 by age 21 would now celebrate her 60th birthday. My mom had not been many places in her life for she'd spent her entire life raising children, grandchildren and yes, even great-grandchildren. Before I continue with her surprise at sixty, allow me to travel back in time a decade earlier.

As a gift to my mother who was now celebrating the big "Five-O", I had flown her out to DC from Cleveland. I then drove her to my place of employment at the time to meet my boss and coworkers. I had already briefed my supervisor about my mother's visit and the surprise that would follow. She would then take my mother to lunch while I continued my workday that would end in a half day. The two of them went to the cafeteria for lunch and after about an hour, my boss explained to her what was to occur. Upon their return, seeing my mom's face soaked with tears, I knew the exchange was a success.

My boss had informed her that there would be a surprise. My supervisor then pulls out two round-trip tickets leaving that next morning for Los Angeles, California where my brother lived. Neither of us had ever been to California and we would both leave together for the fun in the sun. The seven day trip was a total success. Well, I pulled it off! But how would I top that now as a married man with a family? Well, this 60th birthday surprise would far exceed everyone's expectations.

On my Mom's 60th birthday, my wife and I flew her down from, you guessed it -- Cleveland, Ohio. She would be greeted by family and friends. My brother also flew in town from California to join the celebration. As an added surprise, my wife, who's been a liturgical dancer of more than a decade, would gather her church family of sisters and rehearse a routine from the song, *Blessed and Highly Favored* performed by gospel greats, The Clark Sisters.

THE FREEDOM OF GIVING BACK

Fast forward to the night of the event. Our home was filled with family and friends. My wife and group performed a powerful dance interpretation. There wasn't a dry eye in the room. There were words of encouragement by a few speakers. My brother and I spoke as well showing our appreciation for her decision to raise us during a very tough period in our lives. This would be followed by great food, a beautiful birthday cake, pictures and alike. The event was a success, and the evening came to a close. Now comes the added twist!

The following morning as mom began packing for her trip back to Ohio; there would be a pristine, black stretch limo in front of our home to greet her. We thought we would see her off in style. My mom, along with my wife, son, sister-in-law, brother me got in to see her off.

She was really taken aback by all the surprises, but the best was yet to come. As we approached the airport, we provided her with an airline ticket. She was unaware of what was about to happen. Finally, my wife told her that she would set sail on a cruise and requested that she look inside the envelope. Mom looked at her ticket which was accompanied by her cabin number on a 5 night Western Caribbean Cruise. As if that wasn't enough, she was to be accompanied by all passengers of the limo with the exception of me and my brother. All bags and luggage were placed in the limo a block away from the home prior to the driver approaching the property. This was a winner! My mother had never been on a cruise of any kind. For me, this surprise was more gratifying than the trip to sunny California just a decade earlier.

This is a great way to live your life, by adding value to not only yourself but to others as well. Most people come up with ideas only to follow those ideas with excuses as to why they "can't". All it really takes is one decision why you "can". Here's the truth: You're either getting better, or getting worse, there is no such thing as staying the same.

Why Some People Don't Give Back

Have you ever done something nice for someone and got that immense, good, warm-and-fuzzy feeling of having contributed something to the world in general? It would be nice if we could bottle that feeling but it's something that is available to everyone, everyday.

For many people, success comes from giving service to others. If you look at any successful person, they got to where they are for a lot of reasons, but one major reason is that they provide great service to others. Now, that is on a grand scale of course, but the act of giving great service to others is not limited to those with large companies or tons of customers, it is also available to every single person on the planet at all times.

The act of contribution is something that many people have lost, I believe, it's because of the busy lives we lead. Many people don't see how they can possibly give service to others when they can barely get all their own stuff done on a given day.

The reality is that giving or contributing to someone else can be a simple act of kindness that you rarely see in today's society. It needn't take much time. It's an old cliché, but helping an old elderly person across the road is a classic almost everyone can relate to.

Ways to give random acts of kindness are presented to you constantly every day. All it takes is time and when the time is taken to do it, you'll find that you DO get something back. What you get back is a great vibration and goodwill from all over the place. It's not monetary, it's just an amazing feeling. What's also true is that in the bigger picture, the best way to accumulate wealth, happiness, or anything else you desire is to keep the flow going, to pay it forward, to give back, to contribute, to give of yourself. Give back and get more!

So find ways to do it, be open to that, and look for something you can do for someone. Do it and I guarantee you'll feel better about yourself, you'll lift the person you do it for and everyone wins. The vibration will spread to those people and they might feel inspired to do something too. Wow, now we're changing the world! Powerful-- would you agree? Take the first step and start the wave.

Chapter 16

Putting It
All Together

Now that we are at the end of the book, I want to reintroduce myself to you and summarize my life's journey for you.

My name is James J. Williams and together with my wife Greta and our son James, we are living our dreams! My wife and I were always a couple of dreamers. Many years ago, during our courtship, our favorite pastime was driving to new housing developments. We were always taken by the pristine landscape of those neighborhoods. Long before we were married, we would have discussions on the kind of life we wanted for ourselves. In our mid-30s, we had traveled the country at a moments notice like a couple of college hippies. We wanted to see beyond the borders of our residences at the time.

My success and freedom really took shape when I became a father in December 2004 with James's arrival to this planet. It was then that I saw the seeds of being an entrepreneur were sown. The harvest begins with the publication of this book. Why? Well, to answer that, let's take a step back and review.

My previous life was that of work, school, and plenty of obstacles in between. Even today, I have a very successful triple career as IT professional, Warrant Officer in the Army Reserves and might I add, professional student. As a bachelor, my need for achievement, coupled with no other responsibilities was huge. I was quite happy putting in the hours and building my career. Once I found my wife Greta, and became a father, my priorities shifted significantly. I was no longer happy just working a job only to pay bills. It became exhausting and keeping me away from the people I love most. I was away from my family anywhere between nine to eleven hours a day, sometimes six days a week. There just had to be a better way!

Bringing you up to the present, I have now taken the necessary steps of becoming an author, publisher and speaker. In fact, I am so committed to living the life I have now, that working smarter not harder is my only option at this stage in life.

I hope this book has presented some inspiring and helpful tips to assist you on whatever journey you're on. If you're looking for a solution to finding more money, more freedom, more success, a better lifestyle or all of the above then--just do it!"

PUTTING IT ALL TOGETHER

Recipe for Success & Freedom

What made me think of this subject? Believe it or not, sweet potato pie! As the holiday season approach each year, I'm constantly reminded of my grandmother's sweet potato pie. She would only use natural ingredients even down to the crust in which she rolled the flour mixture by hand. Eggs, nutmeg, cinnamon, and molasses were added to provide just the right consistency. There would be no yams from a can in this pie rather boiled sweet potatoes that were mashed or whipped. I know that recipe very well and although I don't claim to be a cook, I believe my results would make my grandmother smile.

How much easier would it have been if she just went to the local market and bought the 'packet mix'? That magical box of pre-made ingredients you just pour into a bowl, add your wet substances like milk and eggs, then whisk and you're done! The problem with that is, although quicker, you don't really know what's gone into the food you're eating. Preservatives? Chemicals? How old were the parts of the 'mix' before they were combined? All this would be a variable – no problem if you don't care what goes into your body I suppose.

I thought about this and saw some parallels in other areas of our lives. Think about success: success is something that can elude some people because they look for the magic dust, the quick formula, the next big instant thing that'll make them successful RIGHT NOW! It's just not that simple. Not only that, but what about all the lessons of creating that success that you'll miss out on if you use the Instant Packet Mix? Entrepreneurs can be successful over and over again because they learn the tough and hard lessons of life and business. They succeed, they fail, but each time they KNOW how to create it again and again. They know and learn more of the secret, tasty, fresh and juicy ingredients that go towards making that success pie.

If you want success in your life, in whatever you choose to do; business, career, sports, whatever – then you absolutely deserve to create that success from scratch. Get all the ingredients together, take your time, and follow the recipe from those great successful business "cooks" that came before you. Study the entrepreneurial master-chefs and how they did it. You'll be setting yourself up with the best recipe for success – because you wrote it.

From Dreaming To Achieving Success & Freedom

Challenge yourself to ask and answer some or all of the following questions to create a snapshot of your level of life satisfaction right now. Know that whether you are extremely happy and satisfied overall or are struggling in most or all areas of your life this process will be a great first step to gaining clarity, which will allow you to know where you may wish to make some adjustments to make your life more powerful and full of joy than ever.

- What are 3 things you love about your life?
- What aspect of your life (faith, work, marriage, parenting, etc) are you most satisfied with?
- What aspect of your life are you most dissatisfied with?
- What is your stress level right now on a scale of 1 to 10?
- Are you always feeling like there are too many things on your plate and almost everything is "urgent"?
- Are you able to focus only on work when you are at work and only on family when you are spending time at home or does stress and concern from one area of your life bleed into another?
- What is missing from your life that you wish were present?
- What do you look forward to every week?
- What things do you dread that are a regular part of your life right now?
- What are 5 things that you are "tolerating" or "putting up with" that are draining your energy?
- How would your life improve if you could resolve/eliminate those "energy drains"?
- Do you feel you have clarity and are living "your calling in life"?
- What have you always dreamed about, but have never done for one reason or another?
- What things do you really enjoy doing for yourself that you no longer make time for in your life?
- Do you compensate for challenges or stress in your personal life and relationships by working harder and achieving more at work?
- Do you believe passionately in what you do and the company you represent assuming you work in a corporate or government setting?
- Are you able to switch gears when you come in your front door after work and focus and enjoy your spouse, children or friends or are you often preoccupied with "critical, urgent issues with your job" that prevent you from smelling the roses of simple moments and blessings of home-life?

PUTTING IT ALL TOGETHER

Just simply completing this exercise and reading this book, you have begun 'chasing the eagle'. You are now on your way to living the formula that has worked for me:

SUCCESS + FREEDOM = FULFILLMENT

Congratulations, and I truly wish you the very best your life has to offer. Now, go *Chase that Eagle!*

Additional
Resources

The following are recommended sources, websites and venues for increased knowledge and enhanced personal development:

THE BEST PLACES TO NETWORK

- Professional conferences
- Volunteer activities
- Gyms and health clubs
- Alumni associations
- Religious institutions and events
- Bookstores

WEBSITES

- Risingeaglepublishing.com
- Frasernet.com
- Parapublishing.com
- Facebook.com
- Linkedin.com

SUGGESTED READING

- *How Successful People Think: Change Your Thinking, Change Your Life* by John C. Maxwell (Zondervan Publishing House, 2009)

- *Self-Improvement 101: What Every Leader Needs to Know* by John C. Maxwell (Zondervan Publishing House, 2009)

- *Believe and Achieve: W Clement Stone's 17 Principles of Success* by Samuel A. Cypert (Avon Books Printing, 1991)

- *The 8th Habit: From Effectiveness to Greatness* by Stephen R. Covey (Free Press, 2004)

- *Click: Ten Truths for Building Extraordinary Relationships* by George C. Fraser (McGraw-Hill, 2008)

- *Good is Not Enough: And Other Unwritten Rules For Minority Professionals* by Keith R. Wyche (Penguin Group, 2008)

ADDITIONAL RESOURCES

- *It Only Takes A Minute to Change Your Life!* By Willie Jolley (St. Martin Press, 1997)

- *Think and Grow Rich* by Napoleon Hill (Ballantine, 1963)

- *Reposition Yourself* by T.D. Jakes (Atria, 2007)

- *The Holy Bible (King James Version)*

MAGAZINES AND NEWSPAPER

- **Daily:** Your local newspaper, *Washington Post, New York Times, and Wall Street Journal*

- **Weekly:** *Time Magazine, Federal Times, Military Times, Newsweek, US News & World Report and Business-Week*

- **Monthly:** *Success Magazine, Entrepreneur, Vetrepreneur, GI Jobs, Black Enterprise, O, Forbes, Money, and Fortune*

Author's Biography

PROFESSIONAL CAREER

James J. Williams' career spans more than 25 years as an Information Technology and Human Resources professional. He's held various mid-to-senior level positions for several Fortune 500 companies including: AT&T, General Electric, General Dynamics and Northrop Grumman. For the past decade, James has tackled progressive responsibilities in the cybersecurity industry. He currently serves as Senior Cybersecurity Analyst at Fort Meade, Maryland. During these tough economic times, James is described among his peers as a *"new voice for career transitioners!"*

CLEVELAND, OHIO - WHERE IT ALL BEGAN...

While James's accomplishments may seem significant, his beginnings were very humble. He was born in Cleveland, Ohio into a family of 4 children. James was the firstborn child having a younger brother and two younger sisters. From grade school through high school, his young life would be dual-hatted as both older brother and as father in a single parent household. Growing up on the streets of Cleveland, the idea of dreaming or achieving didn't seem possible for James. His high school guidance counselor suggested that he attend community college solely based on his economic status. She was not convinced that he was college material. James' faith in God and himself propelled his vision to a different reality.

While a sophomore at John F. Kennedy High School, James was accepted into Cleveland's highly competitive Upward Bound Program which is the oldest series of programs created by President Lyndon B. Johnson's "War on Poverty". Founded in 1964, this program gave participants exposure to a variety of cultural, educational and social experiences.

In 1982, after successfully completing the 2-year program, James would go on to graduate high school and become a scholarship recipient to attend Kent State University. He pursued a degree in Business Administration. After attending for two years, James was accepted to Howard University and in 1985 moved to Washington, DC. However, James would later discover in his junior year that his scholarship funds had depleted. With no other resources available, withdrawing from Howard was his only option.

AUTHOR'S BIOGRAPHY

Soon James found himself working various jobs until he later discovered a second career in the Army Reserves in 1988. This career allowed him to honorably serve his nation while attending college classes using the Montgomery GI Bill. In 1995 while in his senior year, James was nominated and published into the National Dean's List publication for academic excellence. Later that same year, James was inducted into the National Honor Society. In 1996, 14 years post-high school, and at age 31, James would finally earn his Bachelor's degree in Computer Information Systems from Strayer University. The rest, as they say, is history!

EDUCATION

A huge advocate for higher education, James also holds a Masters degree in Public Administration from Strayer University. He is now a doctoral candidate pursuing a PhD in Public Administration and Leadership at Walden University. He is on track with completing his dissertation by summer 2014. James is also a member of the American Society of Public Administration (ASPA).

MILITARY CAREER

After more than 20 years of service, James still enjoys his military reserve career as an Army Chief Warrant Officer in the Adjutant General Corps with no future plans of retirement. A proud member of the U.S. Army Warrant Officer Association, this service member understands there is no greater service than to God and Country! He often echoes these words said by so many others before him:

"Service is the rent we pay for the space we occupy on Earth!"

A selectee for promotion to the rank of CW4, Chief Warrant Officer Williams is assigned to the Headquarters of the United States Pacific Command (USPACOM) located in Camp Smith, Hawaii. He currently serves as the Joint Program Reserve Manager in the Army Reserve Affairs Branch. Throughout his military career, he has been awarded several medals and decorations including: Joint Service Commendation Medal, Joint Service Achievement Medal (2nd award), Army Commendation Medal, Army Achievement Medal, and the Joint Meritorious Unit Award (2nd award).

From Dreaming To Achieving Success & Freedom

RISING EAGLE PUBLISHING, LLC.

James is also the Founder/CEO of Rising Eagle Publishing, LLC a small publishing company designed to discover and promote unknown authors. Rising Eagle Publishing (REP) was established in July 2010 and provides publishing services to aspiring writers and publishers who wish to tap into this $20 billion a year industry. The tagline used "Putting Your Mind on Paper" encourages the desire to transform thoughts to the printed word.

James expanded this new venture as a self-published author of his debut book, *CHASING THE EAGLE: From Dreaming to Achieving Success & Freedom.* Nominated for 6 book awards including Best Inspirational, Best Book Cover and Best New Non-Fiction, this award-winning book is an **absolute must read!** A budding author, publisher, speaker and entrepreneur, James' inspiring talks on success principles, goal setting, and publishing are as popular among college students as they are among corporate and military professionals. James is a proud member of the Independent Book Publishers Association (IBPA).

FAMILY OF FAITH

James also recognizes his greatest accomplishments as husband to his wife Greta and father to their son James II. Upper Marlboro, Maryland residents, the Williams family attend worship service at the First Baptist Church of Glenarden where Pastor John K. Jenkins and First Lady Trina Jenkins serve as senior leaders. A family of faith, the Williams' acknowledge that through Christ:

ALL THINGS ARE POSSIBLE!

For purchases, bookings, speaking engagements, publishing consulting
or other inquires please contact us:

JAMES J. WILLIAMS
Author | Consultant | Speaker | Entrepreneur
www.jamesjosephwilliams.com

Rising Eagle Publishing, LLC
12138 Central Avenue, Suite 102 Bowie, MD 20721
800.828.9414 - O 800.828.9251 - F 301.806.8614-C
www.risingeaglepublishing.com || james@risingeaglepublishing.com